Petite Sweets

Bite-Size Desserts to Satisfy Every Sweet Tooth

BY BEATRICE OJAKANGAS

PHOTOGRAPHS BY ROGER LEPAGE

SELLERS

PUBLISHING

Published by Sellers Publishing, Inc.

Text copyright © 2009 Beatrice Ojakangas
Photographs copyright © 2009 Sellers Publishing, Inc.
All rights reserved.

Sellers Publishing, Inc.
161 John Roberts Road, South Portland, Maine 04106
For ordering information:
(800) 625-3386 toll free
Visit our Web site: www.sellerspublishing.com • E-mail: rsp@rsvp.com

ISBN: 13: 978-1-4162-0773-3
Library of Congress Control Number: 2009923845

10 9 8 7 6 5 4

Printed and bound in China.

CONTENTS

Introduction...4

Basics...7

Little Cakes...10

Petite Pies and Tarts......................................40

Fruit and Berry Desserts...................................60

Mousses and Chilled Desserts...............................80

Creams, Custards, and Frozen Desserts......................96

Pastries and Sweets.......................................122

Index...144

Welcome to Petite Sweets

"Waste not, want not" was the mantra of my mother who lived through the Great Depression. As the oldest of ten, this rubbed off on me, too. I learned it was a "sin" to throw away food, especially dried bread that could be made into bread pudding. I ate so much bread pudding growing up that it has taken me many years to overcome bread pudding fatigue. But lately, bread pudding has crept back into my repertoire because I've learned that the servings don't have to be big, honking globs of bread cubes, barely softened with tasteless custard. Mini bread puddings soft with cream, fruits, nuts, and a bit of spirit baked in little 2-ounce ramekins and served with a spoonful of rich whiskey sauce have changed my mind.

THE DESSERT "SYNDROMES"

Downsizing desserts to bite-size servings solves the problem of the "one and four syndrome" (one dessert and four forks) or the "sliver syndrome" as Chicago Restaurateur Gale Gand put it (I'll have a sliver of this and a sliver of that) and offers your guests neat little one- or two-bite dessert packages. Restaurateurs, too, have found that many diners are looking for "just a little something sweet" to satisfy at the end of the meal. In fact, the top dessert trend today is to downsize desserts. Sweet and rich little cupcakes, a spoonful of banana crème brûlée, a tiny butter-crusted pecan pie or fruit tart, itty-bitty Key lime pies, or a velvety chocolate mousse offered in fun and funky little dishes add to sampling whimsy, and satisfy the desire for a bit of something sweet after a meal.

How to Downsize your Favorite Desserts into Sweet Little Bites

If restaurants can do it with favorite popular desserts — so can we do it at home using our favorite recipes. There is not too much adjusting to be done except that you need to have smaller baking and serving dishes, shorter baking times, and often, it helps to cut a recipe down by half.

Keep your eye out for small dishes that hold less than 4 ounces (½ cup). Look around for small ramekins and cups, especially those that are appropriate for baking. On the Internet, I located small 1- and 2-ounce ramekins, ideal for tiny bites of custards and soufflés. In my local supermarket, I located miniature muffin tins perfect for miniature desserts like cakes and downsized pies. In local restaurant supply stores, I found inexpensive 2-ounce (¼ cup) metal and pottery butter and sauce dishes, ideal for chilled mousses and creamy desserts. Check the housewares sections of department stores for little dishes. I have found interesting pieces of glassware, such as shot glasses, liqueur glasses and cups, and even demitasse cups (which are ideal for little mousses and chilled desserts) at estate sales. When you portion desserts into small dishes, they don't have to all be identical, although they should hold approximately the same amount. A variety of shapes and sizes makes the offering all the more interesting.

There are a few other adjustments you will have to make when preparing petite sweets. When you are using your own favorite recipes, often the amounts need to be halved to keep the yield from being unwieldy. This is helpful when making your favorite cakes and pies to keep the yield numbers reasonable. For baked desserts, small sizes will require less baking time. For starters, cut the baking time in half.

How to Plan the Dessert Menu

When planning the menu, I always like to include something chocolate for the chocoholics. I choose a variety of flavors and textures, from the three basic categories: something chocolate, something pale or white, and some fruit desserts. Always keep in mind that the richer the dessert, the tinier it can be. This saves your guests from having to handle big slices of cakes or pies.

Small bites of dessert are easy to handle, transport, and store. I especially like having lidded containers with square corners to store desserts in the refrigerator or in the freezer. This can be a real bonus when entertaining. With a selection of small desserts carefully packed in freezer containers you can offer a lovely selection quickly with just a last minute garnish or topping. A collection of miniature cream puffs and pastry shells, baked in miniature muffin cups, frozen, can be the basis of a variety of desserts. Most of the desserts in this collection can be frozen with the exception of those that contain gelatin. Gelatin will change in texture when frozen.

BASICS

EQUIPMENT

Measuring cups, both liquid and dry, and measuring spoons are essential. An electronic or kitchen balance scale is very helpful.

Mixing bowls, both metal and glass, in small, medium, and large sizes are useful if not necessary. A handheld electric mixer is great for small amounts of ingredients, and for its portability; however, a stand mixer is most helpful when extended beating is needed. Other helpful mixing tools include wooden spoons for mixing dough, rubber spatulas, a small whisk for mixing small amounts in a small dish, a medium-sized whisk for stirring mixtures in a saucepan, and a balloon whisk for beating larger amounts of egg whites or cream in a large bowl. A food processor or blender is handy for grating, cutting fat into flour, and mixing certain ingredients, although it is not totally necessary.

Knives for cutting and chopping; scrapers for shaving chocolate; peelers for apples and other fruits; zesters for citrus rinds; reamers for extracting juice from lemons, limes, and oranges; sieves for dusting desserts or removing lumps from cocoa and powdered sugar; rolling pins for dough; and scoops of various sizes for portioning dough are in my cabinet.

Parchment paper, waxed paper, foil, and plastic wrap are necessities.

Miniature muffin tins, fluted tart pans, and miniature metal and ceramic dishes are all useful when downsizing desserts. (Look for the kind of mini dishes that restaurants use for serving sauces and butter.) Miniature shot glasses and little dessert dishes for serving rich little desserts can add variety to your dessert display.

Piping bags are useful for decorating desserts. Disposable piping bags are available in craft stores, and a variety of tips are nice to have. You can also use a heavy-duty plastic bag with the corner snipped off to decorate desserts.

INGREDIENTS

Butter or fat: There is no substitute for the flavor of butter. Whether it is lightly salted or unsalted, butter is always preferred in these recipes, unless the recipe specifically calls for oil. Generally, butter needs to be softened before being creamed into a mixture. For pastries, butter should be chilled in order to be "cut" into flour. Sometimes a recipe calls for melted butter. Recipes in this book were not tested with margarine for both health and performance reasons.

Cream: Heavy cream and whipping cream can be used interchangeably. Heavy cream (sometimes labeled as heavy whipping cream) has a slightly higher fat content (36 percent to 42 percent fat). Dairies often add carrageenan to whipping cream (35 percent fat) to stabilize the cream and to assist in the ability to whip the cream. Light whipping cream has between 30 percent and 36 percent fat.

You can use any of these products in *Petite Sweets* recipes that call for whipping cream, as long as the recipe calls for whipping the cream and the cream you have will whip successfully. The difference in the end product will be in flavor and calories.

Sugar: In this book we have used granulated white sugar, superfine (castor) sugar, light and dark brown sugar, powdered sugar, pure maple syrup, and light and dark corn syrup. Although the recipes were not tested with sugar substitutes, many recipes could be sweetened with them.

Flour: Plain all-purpose flour, as opposed to self-rising flour, was used here. Self-rising flour has salt and a leavening agent added.

Eggs: All of the recipes in this book were tested with large eggs. When a recipe requires just the yolks, we refrigerated the whites. When a recipe calls for just whites, you can use the whites, just measure ½ cup egg white to equal 4 egg whites. To bring eggs to room temperature, place in a bowl of warm water for 2–3 minutes.

Flavorings: Chocolate, vanilla, almond, and spices constitute a category by themselves. Chocolate can be unsweetened, semisweet, bittersweet, milk chocolate, or white chocolate, and it comes in blocks or in bits. Generally, chocolate chips (or bits) can be substituted for semisweet, bittersweet, or milk chocolate in a recipe. When using cocoa, be sure that it is not sweetened. Vanilla should be pure vanilla extract as opposed to artificially flavored vanilla. Almond extract also should be pure, not artificially flavored. Check your spices, as they can lose flavor over time. Always use fresh ingredients.

Fruits and berries: When using fresh fruits and berries, the most flavorful are always those that are in season. Dried fruits like raisins, cranberries, apricots, and prunes are always in season, but they don't last forever. Be sure to use them before their expiration date.

CHOCOLATE VELVET CAKES

FRESH GINGER CARROT CAKELETS

ANGEL CAKES WITH LEMON SAUCE

CARDAMOM-SPICED CURRANT CAKES

COCONUT RUM BUTTER CAKES

SPONGE CAKE

MINI CHEESECAKES WITH
BERRIES AND FRUIT

COFFEE CHOCOLATE (DOBOS TORTE) ROLLS

BABY RUM BABAS

WHOOPIE PIES

BITTERSWEET ESPRESSO
CHOCOLATE BROWNIE BITES

Little Cakes

The recipes in this chapter showcase everyday favorites like chocolate, carrot, and angel cakes, as well as those you might not have thought would be this easy to make. Made in petite versions, they make many servings, even though most of the recipes have been cut in volume from the original.

CHOCOLATE VELVET CAKES

Red Velvet Cake is a "Southern" chocolate favorite. Some time in the 1940s, a story circulated about a woman who had dined at New York's elegant Waldorf-Astoria and had asked for the recipe. According to the tale, a short time later they sent her a bill for $100. The angry woman with revenge in mind began circulating the recipe along with her story. To make Red Velvet Cake, add 1 tablespoon red food coloring to the cake batter. Here we've made the cake into tiny bite-size portions and eliminated the food coloring. The acid of the buttermilk combined with cocoa powder brings forward a reddish color.

MAKES 24

4 tablespoons (½ stick) unsalted butter
¾ cup sugar
1 large egg, at room temperature
2 tablespoons unsweetened cocoa powder
1¼ cups all-purpose flour
½ teaspoon salt
½ teaspoon baking soda
½ cup buttermilk
1½ teaspoons white vinegar
1 teaspoon pure vanilla extract
Vanilla Frosting (recipe follows)

Chopped toasted walnuts (optional for garnish)

Preheat oven to 350°F. Coat 24 miniature muffin cups with nonstick cooking spray or line with miniature paper liners.

Cream butter and add the sugar; beat until light and fluffy. Beat in the egg and mix in the cocoa. In a small bowl, mix the flour, salt, and baking soda. In a 1-cup measure, mix the buttermilk, vinegar, and vanilla.

continues

Add the dry ingredients to the creamed mixture alternately with the buttermilk mixture. Beat until batter is smooth and fluffy. Spoon the batter into the prepared muffin cups, dividing equally. The batter will come nearly to the top of each cup. Bake for 12–15 minutes or until cakes feel firm when touched in the center. Remove from the oven and cool.

Vanilla Frosting:

3 tablespoons all-purpose flour
½ cup milk
1 cup powdered sugar
8 tablespoons (1 stick) butter
1 teaspoon pure vanilla extract

In a small saucepan, combine the flour and milk. Cook over medium heat, stirring constantly until thickened. Cover and chill. In a medium-sized bowl, beat the sugar, butter, and vanilla until thick and light. Add the chilled flour mixture to the creamed mixture and blend until smooth.

Frost each cooled cake and dip into chopped walnuts, if desired.

FRESH GINGER CARROT CAKELETS

Carrot cake is notoriously rich, which is probably why it is so loved! But, just like any other really rich dessert, a bite is a feast! This downsized version is about half the size of the original recipe. Bake these in paper-lined miniature muffin tins.

MAKES 36

Cakelets:
1 cup all-purpose flour
1 cup sugar
1 teaspoon baking powder
½ teaspoon salt
2 large eggs, at room temperature
1½ cups finely shredded carrots
⅓ cup milk
⅓ cup canola or vegetable oil
2 teaspoons grated fresh gingerroot
½ cup finely chopped pecans or walnuts, toasted

Cream Cheese Frosting (recipe follows)

Toasted pecan or walnut halves (for garnish)

Preheat the oven to 350°F. Line 36 miniature muffin cups with paper liners. Coat the paper liners with cooking spray.

In a large bowl, stir together the flour, sugar, baking powder, and salt. In another bowl, beat the eggs; then stir in the carrots, milk, oil, ginger, and pecans. Stir the liquid ingredients into the dry ingredients.

Divide batter between the 36 lined cups. Bake for 14–15 minutes or until centers of cakes feel firm to the touch. Remove from the oven and cool.

continues

Cream Cheese Frosting:

1 (3-ounce) package cream cheese, softened
1 cup powdered sugar
4 tablespoons (½ stick) butter
1 teaspoon grated orange zest

To prepare the frosting, beat the cream cheese, powdered sugar, butter, and orange zest together until smooth.

Spread frosting on the cooled cakes and top with the toasted pecan halves.

ANGEL CAKES WITH LEMON SAUCE

If you have them, bake these cakes in either round or heart-shaped pans with removable bottoms. If not, you can use 24 regular-sized muffin pans. Serve them with the Lemon Sauce.

MAKES 24

Cakes:

½ cup cake flour, sifted before measuring
⅔ cup sugar, divided
6 large egg whites, room temperature
¾ teaspoon cream of tartar
⅛ teaspoon salt
½ teaspoon lemon extract

Lemon Sauce (recipe follows)

Preheat the oven to 325°F. Have 24 muffin cups ready, preferably with removable bottoms. If not, cut 24 rounds of parchment or waxed paper to fit the bottoms of regular muffin cups. Do not grease.

In a small bowl, stir the cake flour and ⅓ cup of the sugar together. Set aside. In a large bowl, stir together the egg whites, cream of tartar, salt, and lemon extract. With a hand mixer, beat the egg whites until frothy. Slowly add the remaining ⅓ cup sugar and continue beating at a high speed until whites are stiff but not dry.

Using a rubber spatula, fold in the flour mixture until completely incorporated. Divide the cake batter between the muffin cups.

Bake for 10–12 minutes or until the cakes feel dry when touched in the center. Remove from the oven and cool.

continues

Lemon Sauce:

½ cup sugar
1 tablespoon cornstarch
⅛ teaspoon salt
1 cup boiling water
1 tablespoon butter
1 teaspoon grated lemon zest
Juice of 1 lemon

To prepare the sauce, stir together the sugar, cornstarch, and salt in a large saucepan. Gradually stir in boiling water, and simmer over low heat until thick, stirring occasionally.

Remove from heat; stir in butter, lemon zest, and lemon juice. Turn into a metal bowl, cover with plastic wrap, and chill.

To serve, loosen edges of cakes with the tip of a thin knife and lift cakes out of the pans. Arrange on a serving platter and spoon the sauce over each cake.

CARDAMOM-SPICED CURRANT CAKES

My friend, Leila, in Helsinki, makes these delicious little cakes and serves them with coffee after guests have had a sauna. She bakes them in little fluted metal tins called sandbakkel. Sandbakkel tins are available in Scandinavian gift shops as well as online.

MAKES 36

Cakes:

8 tablespoons (1 stick) butter, softened
½ cup sugar
4 large eggs, at room temperature
1 teaspoon freshly crushed cardamom seeds
½ cup currants
1 cup all-purpose flour
½ teaspoon baking powder

Sugar Topping (recipe follows)

Preheat the oven to 375°F. Coat 36 small (1½ to 2-inch) fluted sandbakkel tins or fluted molds with cooking spray.

In a mixing bowl, cream the butter and sugar until blended and smooth. Whisk in the eggs one at a time until mixture is light. Add the cardamom and currants. Stir the flour and baking powder together and add to the mixture. Beat on high speed for about 5 minutes, until batter is very light.

Spoon the mixture into the prepared tins, dividing the dough evenly. Place on a baking sheet and bake for 12–15 minutes or until golden. Remove cakes from the tins and cool on waxed paper.

continues

Sugar Topping:
¼ cup powdered sugar
Few drops water
Pearl sugar*

To garnish the cakes, in a small bowl mix the powdered sugar with enough water to make a thin glaze. Brush the bottoms of the cakes with the glaze and dip into the pearl sugar to decorate.

*Pearl sugar is a coarse white sugar widely used in Scandinavian baking. It can be purchased on line or in Scandinavian and Finnish specialty shops. Crushed sugar cubes make an adequate substitute.

COCONUT RUM BUTTER CAKES

These Caribbean-inspired cakes are pretty when baked in miniature bundt pans (¼-cup capacity). As an alternative, you can bake these cakes in a regular-sized muffin tin. This recipe will fill 12 miniature bundt pans.

MAKES 12

Cake:

Melted butter and flour for pans
⅓ cup buttermilk
1 tablespoon coconut rum
1 cup all-purpose flour
½ teaspoon baking powder
¼ teaspoon baking soda
¼ teaspoon salt
5 tablespoons butter
½ cup sugar
2 large eggs, at room temperature

Coconut Rum Sauce (recipe follows)

Toasted coconut, fresh raspberries, or powdered sugar (optional, for garnish)

Preheat oven to 325° F. Brush the bottoms of 12 miniature bundt pans with melted butter and dust with flour.

In a 1-cup measure, combine buttermilk and coconut rum. In a small bowl, stir the flour, baking powder, baking soda, and salt together; sift and then set aside. In a medium mixing bowl, cream butter and sugar; beat in eggs until light and fluffy. Stir in the buttermilk mixture, then the flour mixture until batter is smooth.

Divide batter between the cups. Bake for 20–30 minutes or until cakes feel firm when touched. Prepare the Coconut Rum Sauce while the cakes are baking.

continues

Coconut Rum Sauce:

½ cup sugar
½ cup water
1 tablespoon butter
4 tablespoons coconut rum

For the Coconut Rum Sauce, combine sugar, water, and butter over medium-high heat. Bring to a boil. Remove from heat. Stir in rum.

While cakes are still warm, pierce several times with bamboo skewers or a fork, and drench with half of the hot sauce. Remove from pans after cakes have cooled and spoon remaining sauce over cakes.

Before serving, garnish with toasted coconut, fresh raspberries, or lightly dust with powdered sugar.

SPONGE CAKE

This simple sponge cake is used in the Strawberry Bruschetta on page 74 of the Fruit and Berry Desserts. It makes a perfect base for shortcakes, and it also can be cut into squares or rounds and dried to make rusks. The rusks keep well and can be served like a cookie, or used in place of ladyfingers in desserts.

MAKES ONE 9 X 13-INCH LAYER CAKE

3 large eggs, at room temperature
⅔ cup sugar
Pinch of salt
1 teaspoon pure vanilla extract
⅔ cup all-purpose flour

Preheat the oven to 350°F. Line the bottom of a 9 x 13-inch baking pan with parchment paper.

In the large bowl of an electric mixer, beat the eggs until foamy. Turn speed to high and gradually add the sugar; beat for about 5 minutes until mixture is very light and thick; then add the pinch of salt and vanilla. Turn speed to low and slowly add the flour, mixing until the flour is incorporated.

Turn the mixture into the prepared baking pan and spread evenly to the edges. Bake for 20–25 minutes or until the center of the cake springs back when touched. Remove from the oven and cool.

Use cake as directed in recipes requiring a sponge cake. To make sweet rusks, cut the cake into 2-inch squares or rounds and split horizontally. Place on a baking sheet and dry in a 300°F oven for 10–15 minutes or until rusks are dry. Store in an airtight container.

MINI CHEESECAKES WITH BERRIES AND FRUIT

A vanilla wafer is the ready-made bottom crust of these little cheesecakes.

MAKES 24

24 vanilla wafers
2 (8-ounce) packages cream cheese, softened
½ cup sugar
1 tablespoon all-purpose flour
1–2 tablespoons light rum, liqueur, or apple juice
1 teaspoon pure vanilla extract
2 large eggs, at room temperature

Fruit Topping (recipe follows)

Preheat the oven to 325°F. Lightly spray a mini cheesecake pan with cooking spray or line a standard muffin pan with foil liners or double paper liners. Place a vanilla wafer into each pan or cup.

In a large bowl, with a hand mixer, beat the cream cheese, sugar, flour, rum, and vanilla until well blended. Beat in the eggs until light and fluffy. Divide mixture between the muffin cups. Bake 20–25 minutes or until cheesecakes feel firm in the center. Do not overbake. Remove from pan when cool. Chill.

Fruit Topping:

Fresh raspberries, blueberries, strawberries, peach slices, or cherries
½ cup sugar
2 tablespoons water

As cheesecakes chill, prepare and clean the berries or fruits. Put sugar and water into a small saucepan and bring to a boil. Stir until sugar is dissolved. Cool until warm.

Just before serving, top with your choice of berries or fruit and drizzle with the warm light syrup.

COFFEE CHOCOLATE (DOBOS TORTE) ROLLS

The inspiration for this mini dessert is the classic Dobos Torte of Austria, which is traditionally made of seven thin layers of cake spread with a coffee and chocolate filling. This recipe makes one thin cake, filled with the classic filling, rolled up. The batter for this cake is simple to make and bakes for fewer than 10 minutes. While the cake bakes, you need to make the filling so that it is ready to spread on the warm cake before turning it into a roll.

MAKES 8 SERVINGS

Cake:

2 large eggs, separated, at room temperature
½ cup sifted powdered sugar
¼ cup all-purpose flour
3 tablespoons milk

Chocolate Filling (recipe follows)

Caramel Drizzle (recipe follows)

Chocolate Drizzle (recipe follows)

Preheat the oven to 375°F. Cover the bottom of an 11 x 15-inch jelly roll pan with parchment or waxed paper. Coat with nonstick spray and dust lightly with flour.

In a medium-sized bowl, with a hand mixer, beat the egg whites until stiff but not dry. In another medium bowl, using the same mixer, beat the yolks and slowly add the powdered sugar; continue beating until thick and satiny. Beat in the flour and milk until batter is smooth. Fold this mixture into the beaten egg whites.

Spread the batter evenly over the parchment. Bake for 5–6 minutes or until lightly browned. Loosen cake from the parchment paper. With a knife cut away the crispy edges from the cake.

continues

Chocolate Filling:

1 cup semisweet chocolate chips
¼ cup strong, hot coffee
8 tablespoons (1 stick) butter, soft

While the cake bakes, stir the chocolate and coffee together until chocolate is melted. Stir in the soft butter until mixture is smooth.

Spread the warm baked cake with the chocolate filling and carefully roll up the cake starting from a long side to make a tight roll. Remove rolled cake from pan and cool until firm.

Caramel Drizzle:

½ cup sugar
½ cup whipping cream
1 teaspoon pure vanilla extract
1 teaspoon dark corn syrup

To make the Caramel Drizzle, combine sugar and whipping cream and bring to a boil over medium heat, stirring often. Boil for 5 minutes until slightly thickened. Stir in vanilla and dark corn syrup.

Chocolate Drizzle:

½ cup whipping cream
1 cup semisweet chocolate chips
1 tablespoon light or dark corn syrup

To make the Chocolate Drizzle, bring whipping cream to a boil over medium heat. Remove from heat and add chocolate chips and light or dark corn syrup. Stir until smooth.

To serve, cut roll into 8 equal pieces. Drizzle each serving plate with caramel and chocolate. Place cake rolls on the plates with the cut side up.

BABY RUM BABAS

Rum baba or baba au rhum is a small yeast cake saturated in a liquor-flavored syrup, usually rum. The modern version was invented in France in the early 1800s. Typically it is baked in forms about 2 inches tall. These babas are smaller and bake perfectly in miniature muffin pans. Although this sounds like a difficult, fancy dessert, it is really very simple. The rolls can be refrigerated or frozen. If frozen, thaw in a slow oven (300°F) for a few minutes and serve them warm.

MAKES 36

Babas:

Melted butter and granulated sugar for muffin cups
1 package active dry yeast
¼ cup warm water, 105°F to 115°F
¼ cup lukewarm milk
5 tablespoons butter, melted
2 tablespoons sugar
2 teaspoons grated lemon zest
¼ teaspoon salt
4 large eggs, at room temperature
2 cups all-purpose flour
¼ cup golden raisins
¼ cup currants

Rum Syrup (recipe follows)

Whipped cream (optional, for serving)

Butter and sugar 36 miniature muffin cups.

continues

In a small bowl, combine the yeast and the warm water; let sit until yeast begins to foam (about 5 minutes). Stir in the milk, butter, sugar, lemon zest, and salt. In the large bowl of an electric mixer, beat the eggs and add the yeast mixture. Gradually beat in the flour, mixing until the batter is smooth. Stir in the raisins and currants.

Spoon the batter into the prepared muffin cups. Let rise, uncovered, in a warm place until almost doubled, 30–45 minutes.

Preheat the oven to 375°F. Bake for 10–12 minutes or until a wooden toothpick inserted into the center of one baba comes out clean and dry. As the babas bake, prepare the Rum Syrup.

Rum Syrup:

2 cups sugar
1 cup water
4-inch strip lemon zest
½ cup dark rum

In a small saucepan, bring the sugar, water, and lemon zest to a boil. Boil about 6 minutes to make a thick syrup. Remove from heat and stir in the rum.

Loosen the hot babas from the muffin cups and place them in a rimmed pan. Spoon the prepared syrup over them until they are saturated. Serve immediately, or to store, cover babas in pan and refrigerate or freeze. Before serving, warm in a slow oven for a few minutes. Serve with whipped cream if desired.

WHOOPIE PIES

These are made of two soft chocolate cookies sandwiched with a sweet creamy filling. They are well-known in the eastern U.S., especially Pennsylvania Dutch and Amish areas and New England. Although the traditional pies are made with shortening, I use unsalted butter here for healthful reasons.

MAKES 30

Cookies:

2 cups all-purpose flour
½ cup unsweetened cocoa powder
1 teaspoon baking soda
½ teaspoon salt
1 cup buttermilk
1 teaspoon pure vanilla extract
8 tablespoons (1 stick) unsalted butter, softened
1 cup sugar
1 large egg, at room temperature

Marshmallow Filling (recipe follows)

Preheat oven to 350°F. Butter 2 large cookie sheets.

Whisk together flour, cocoa, baking soda, and salt in a bowl until combined. In a separate small bowl, stir together buttermilk and vanilla.

In a large bowl with an electric mixer beat together butter and sugar at medium-high speed until mixture is pale and fluffy (about 3 minutes in a standing mixer or 5 minutes with a hand mixer). Add egg, beating until combined. Reduce speed to low and alternately mix in flour mixture and buttermilk in batches, beginning and ending with flour, scraping down side of bowl after each flour addition, and mixing until smooth.

continues

Spoon 1-tablespoon mounds of batter onto 2 large buttered cookie sheets. Bake until tops are puffed and cookies spring back when touched, 8–10 minutes. Transfer to a rack to cool completely.

Marshmallow Filling:

8 tablespoons (1 stick) unsalted butter, softened
1¼ cups powdered sugar
2 cups marshmallow cream such as Marshmallow Fluff
1 teaspoon pure vanilla extract

For the filling, beat together butter, powdered sugar, marshmallow cream, and vanilla in a bowl with electric mixer at medium speed until smooth, about 3 minutes.

To assemble the pies, spread a rounded teaspoonful of filling on flat side of half of the cookies and top with remaining cookies. Store in an airtight container; can be well wrapped and frozen for up to 2 months. Bring frozen Whoopie Pies to room temperature before serving.

BITTERSWEET ESPRESSO CHOCOLATE BROWNIE BITES

Bake these deep, dark chocolate brownies in miniature muffin tins lined with paper cups.

MAKES 24

Brownies:
½ cup dark corn syrup
½ cup butter
6 ounces bittersweet chocolate, cut up
¾ cup sugar
3 large eggs, at room temperature
1 cup all-purpose flour
1 teaspoon pure vanilla extract

Espresso-Chocolate Frosting (recipe follows)

Preheat the oven to 325°F. Line 24 miniature muffin cups with paper liners. Coat liners with cooking spray. In a 2-quart saucepan, combine corn syrup, butter, chocolate, and sugar. Place over low heat, stir until the chocolate is melted. Beat in eggs, one at a time, and add the flour and vanilla, mixing until batter is smooth and shiny. Divide batter between the lined muffin cups. Bake for 15–20 minutes or just until a toothpick inserted into the center of one brownie comes out clean. Cool completely.

Espresso-Chocolate Frosting:
½ cup whipping cream
1 tablespoon instant espresso coffee powder
6 squares (6 ounces) bittersweet chocolate, broken up
1 teaspoon pure vanilla extract

For the frosting, in a small saucepan, heat the cream just to simmering. Remove from heat and add the espresso powder and chocolate. Stir until chocolate is melted and mixture is smooth. Add the vanilla. Cool 5 minutes. Spread over the cooled brownies. Chill until firm.

FRESH LIME PIES

VANILLA BANANA
CREAM PIES

MAPLE PECAN PIES

CHOCOLATE TRUFFLE TARTS

MINI MINCE PIES

PETITE LEMON MERINGUE PIES

SWEDISH ALMOND TARTS
(SANDBAKKELSER)

Petite Pies and Tarts

These little pies look and taste like big pies, but they are just
one flavor-packed bite each. They vary from pastry-based little
treats that you can pick up with your fingers to those that you
eat with a tiny spoon from a pretty little glass.

FRESH LIME PIES

You can line miniature muffin tins with foil liners or use 2-ounce ceramic cups, which you do not need to line. If you are lucky enough to find fresh Key limes (peak season June through August), use the juice in these pies. Key limes are yellow when ripe, and smaller and more rounded than the common limes we find in our produce markets. Key limes have a higher acidity and a stronger aroma.

MAKES 24 (2-OUNCE) SERVINGS

Crumb Crust:

5 double graham crackers (10 squares), finely crushed
2 tablespoons sugar
4 tablespoons (½ stick) butter

Lime Filling (recipe follows)

Topping (recipe follows)

Lime zest (for garnish)

Put graham cracker crumbs, sugar, and butter into a heavy nonstick skillet over medium heat. Stir and toast until lightly browned.

Line 24 miniature muffin cups with fluted foil liners or use 24 (2-ounce) unlined ceramic cups. Divide crumb mixture between the cups and tamp down firmly using a spoon or some other tool with a flat end.

Preheat the oven to 350°F.

continues

Lime Filling:

2 large egg yolks
1 (14-ounce) can sweetened condensed milk
½ cup fresh lime juice
2 teaspoons grated lime zest (green portion only)

In a glass 2-cup measure, mix the egg yolks, milk, lime juice, and lime zest until well blended. Pour mixture into the crumb-lined cups, filling them to the very top.

Bake for 15–20 minutes or until set. Cool thoroughly, then chill.

Topping:

½ cup whipping cream
2 teaspoons sugar
¼ teaspoon pure vanilla extract

Just before serving, whip the cream and add the sugar and vanilla. Spoon the whipped cream over each little pie. Garnish with lime zest.

VANILLA BANANA CREAM PIES

The yield here depends on the size of the dishes you use. With 2-ounce stemmed glasses, you will have approximately 12 desserts. We made the filling recipe twice and added chocolate to one batch for the photo. Use the egg yolks in the vanilla cream and the whites for the meringues. The meringues can be made in advance and will keep for months in an airtight container.

MAKES 12 (2-OUNCE) SERVINGS

Crispy Meringues:

2 large egg whites (save yolks for the Vanilla Cream Filling)
4 tablespoons sugar
Pinch of cream of tartar
1 teaspoon pure vanilla extract

Vanilla Cream Filling (recipe follows)

1 ripe but firm banana
12 purchased vanilla wafers (for pie bases)

Preheat the oven to 300°F. Cover a baking sheet with parchment paper.

In a medium-sized metal bowl, whisk the egg whites, sugar, cream of tartar, and vanilla until stiff and glossy. Spoon or pipe the mixture onto the prepared baking sheet to make 1-inch meringues. Bake about 30 minutes or until meringues are dry and lightly browned. Store in an airtight container until ready to use.

continues

Vanilla Cream Filling:

2 cups whole milk
½ cup sugar
3 tablespoons all-purpose flour
Pinch of salt
2 large egg yolks, slightly beaten
1 tablespoon butter
1 teaspoon pure vanilla extract

In a medium-sized saucepan, heat the milk to scalding. In a small bowl, mix the sugar, flour, and a pinch of salt.

Gradually whisk the dry mixture into the hot milk. Stirring occasionally, cook another 2 or 3 minutes over medium heat until pudding is thickened.

Whisk the egg yolks in a small bowl. Whisk a small amount of the hot mixture into the eggs, then stir this into the hot mixture. Cook 1 minute longer over low heat. Remove from the heat and blend in the butter and vanilla. Cool completely, covered.

Just before serving, assemble the pies: Cut the banana into ⅛-inch-thick slices. Place 1 vanilla wafer into each of 12 (2-ounce) little stemmed glasses. Top each wafer with a small spoonful of the Vanilla Cream Filling. Top with 2 or 3 thin slices of banana. Top with another small spoonful of the Vanilla Cream Filling. Top each dessert with a baked meringue.

VARIATION:

Chocolate Banana Cream Pies:
Add 2 ounces bittersweet chocolate, broken up, to the hot filling along with the vanilla. Stir until chocolate is melted.

MAPLE PECAN PIES

Bake these tasty pies in miniature muffin pans.

MAKES 24

Cream Cheese Pastry:

4 ounces (½ of an 8-ounce package) cream cheese, softened
4 tablespoons (½ stick) butter, softened
1 cup all-purpose flour

Maple Pecan Filling (recipe follows)

In a food processor with the steel blade in place, combine cream cheese and butter. Process until blended. Add the flour and process until flour is worked into the mixture. Cover and chill for 30 minutes.

Preheat the oven to 375°F. Divide dough into 24 equal pieces. Place one piece of dough into each of 24 miniature muffin cups. Press dough into bottom and up the sides of the cups to form shells.

Maple Pecan Filling:

1 large egg
¼ cup pure maple syrup
½ cup packed brown sugar
1 teaspoon pure vanilla extract
¾ cup pecans, chopped to ¼-inch pieces

In a small bowl, mix the egg, maple syrup, brown sugar, vanilla, and pecans. Spoon mixture into the muffin cups, dividing the mixture evenly. Bake for 25–30 minutes or until lightly browned. Let stand 5 minutes. Run knife around the edges of each to remove from pans, and serve.

CHOCOLATE TRUFFLE TARTS

Over the years I have collected miniature tart pans in various shapes, but none of them more than 2½ inches in diameter. Lined with butter pastry, the baked shells can be made ahead and frozen until you are ready to fill them with the rich Chocolate Truffle Filling.

MAKES 24

Tart Pastry:

1½ cups all-purpose flour
¼ cup sugar
8 tablespoons (1 stick) unsalted butter, cut up
1 large egg yolk
2 teaspoons lemon juice
2–3 tablespoons ice water

Chocolate Truffle Filling (recipe follows)

Chocolate curls* and a dusting of powdered sugar (for garnish)

Preheat the oven to 400°F.

In a medium-sized mixing bowl, or in a food processor with the steel blade in place, combine the flour and sugar. Add the butter pieces and process using on/off bursts until the butter is totally worked into the flour mixture. Mix the egg yolk, lemon juice, and ice water and stir or process until a dough is formed.

Coat 24 tart pans, each no larger than 2½ inches in diameter, with cooking spray.

Place dough between sheets of waxed paper or plastic wrap. With a rolling pin, roll dough out to about ¼-inch thickness. Using a tart pan as you would a cookie cutter, press into the dough.

continues

Lift cutout of dough and, with fingers, press the dough into the tart pan until it comes up to the top edge. Place filled tart pans on a baking sheet. When all tart pans are filled, bake for 15–18 minutes or until lightly browned.

Remove from oven and cool. Tart shells can be wrapped and frozen until later.

Chocolate Truffle Filling:
½ cup whipping cream
2 tablespoons unsalted butter
1 tablespoon light corn syrup
6 ounces bittersweet or semisweet chocolate

For the filling, place whipping cream, butter, and corn syrup into a small saucepan. Bring to a boil, stirring, then remove from heat. Break the chocolate into pieces and add to the hot cream. Stir about 1 minute until the chocolate is melted and blended into the cream. Allow filling to cool to room temperature.

To serve, spoon or pipe the chocolate filling into each shell. Garnish with a chocolate curl and a dusting of powdered sugar.

*Easy chocolate curls: Place an 8-ounce bar of milk chocolate under a lamp for 5–10 minutes. Pull a cheese scraper across the top to make curls.

MINI MINCE PIES

A classic holiday dessert in England, these miniature pies freeze and keep beautifully. Offer with a selection of desserts, keeping in mind variety in color, shape, and flavor.

MAKES 24

Almond Pastry:

2½ cups all-purpose flour, plus extra for dusting
½ cup ground almonds
12 tablespoons (1½ sticks) butter, cut into small pieces, plus extra for greasing
½ cup superfine sugar
Grated zest of ½ lemon
4–6 tablespoons ice water

Mincemeat Filling (recipe follows)

Decorative Icing (recipe follows)

Preheat the oven to 400° F. Have ready a 24-cup nonstick miniature muffin pan.

Measure flour and almonds into a food processor with the steel blade in place. Process, then blend in the butter. Add the sugar and lemon zest. Process to blend. Turn the crumbly mixture into a large bowl. Sprinkle with the ice water and mix with a fork until dough comes together in a ball. Shape into a flat disk, wrap, and chill 30 minutes.

Roll out dough on a lightly floured surface and using a 3-inch-round cookie cutter cut out 24 circles of pastry. Reserve the remaining pastry dough.

Gently press the pastry circles into the bottom and up the sides of miniature muffin cups.

continues

Mincemeat Filling:

1 cup (8 ounces) almond paste or marzipan
1 cup prepared mincemeat

For the filling, cut the marzipan into 24 small pieces, roll into balls, and then flatten with your hand. Place a piece of marzipan into each pastry-lined cup and top with a teaspoonful of mincemeat.

Reroll the remaining pastry and cut out 1½-inch circles. Cover each pie with these smaller pastry circles and gently press to seal around the edges. Place muffin pans in the center of the oven and bake for 15–20 minutes, or until golden-brown. Tops may open up a little during baking. Remove from the oven and allow to cool in the pans.

Decorative Icing:

1 cup powdered sugar
1½–2 tablespoons warm water
1 teaspoon pure vanilla extract
½ teaspoon pure almond extract

Once the mince pies are cool, mix together the powdered sugar, water, vanilla, and almond extract in a bowl. Drizzle the pies with the icing in a zigzag pattern, and serve.

PETITE LEMON MERINGUE PIES

These bite-size lemon meringue pies are encased in a slightly sweetened buttery pastry and simply filled with lemon curd — purchased or your own homemade version.

MAKES 24

Pastry:
1½ cups all-purpose flour
4 tablespoons (½ stick) unsalted butter, cut up
2 teaspoons sugar
½ teaspoon salt
1 large egg yolk
1 teaspoon lemon juice
2–4 tablespoons ice water

Lemon Filling (recipe follows)

Meringue (recipe follows)

Preheat the oven to 400°F. Have available a 24-cup nonstick miniature muffin pan.

For the pastry, measure the flour into a food processor with the steel blade in place. Add the butter, sugar, and salt. Process with on/off bursts until the mixture resembles coarse meal, 8–10 seconds. Turn mixture into a mixing bowl. In a separate bowl, mix the egg yolk, lemon juice, and ice water. Sprinkle liquid mixture over the dry ingredients and toss with two forks until the dough holds together without being wet or sticky. Shape into a ball, kneading with a few strokes if necessary. Flatten into a disk. Wrap and chill for 30 minutes.

On a floured board, roll the dough out to about ⅛-inch thickness. With a 3-inch-round cookie cutter, cut rounds and fit into the muffin cups. Pierce bottoms with a fork. Bake for 8–10 minutes or until edges are lightly browned. Cool before filling.

continues

Lemon Filling:

1 cup (8 ounces) mascarpone cheese, at room temperature
1 cup prepared lemon curd

For the filling, beat the mascarpone and lemon curd together until smooth. Spoon about 1 tablespoon of the mixture into each of the baked pie shells. Preheat oven to 350°F.

Meringue:

2 large egg whites, at room temperature
¼ cup sugar

In a medium-sized bowl, beat the egg whites until frothy. Gradually beat in the sugar until mixture is glossy and meringue-like. Spoon or pipe the meringue onto each pie. Bake for 8–10 minutes or until just lightly browned. Cool and serve.

SWEDISH ALMOND TARTS (SANDBAKKELSER)

These are little tarts that are baked in small fluted sandbakkel tins, preferably 1½–2 inches in diameter. They are small enough to be served as cookies, but large enough to fill with a dab of jam, jelly, or whipped cream.

MAKES 48

12 tablespoons (1½ sticks) butter, at room temperature
⅔ cup sugar
1 cup blanched almonds, pulverized or ground
1 teaspoon pure almond extract
1 large egg, at room temperature
2 cups all-purpose flour
About 1 cup berry preserves, jam, or jelly
Lightly sweetened whipped cream

In a large bowl, cream the butter and sugar until well blended and light. Blend in the almonds, almond extract, and egg. Stir in the flour. Turn dough out onto a lightly floured surface and knead briefly until the dough forms a smooth ball. Add a bit more flour if needed to make a stiff dough. Gather into a ball, wrap, and chill for 30 minutes.

Preheat the oven to 375°F. Lightly butter or coat with nonstick spray 4 dozen fluted sandbakkel tins or tart tins. Pinch off parts of the dough and, using your thumb, press into the tart pans to make a thin, even layer. Place filled tins on a baking sheet for easier handling. Bake for 12–15 minutes or until golden. Remove tarts from oven and let cool in tins.

To remove the tins, gently tap the tin until the tart comes out. Serve unfilled (upside down on a serving plate to reveal the impression from the pan), or invert the tart shells so that the cavity is upright. Just before serving, spoon berry preserves, jam, or jelly into the cavity and top with a small dollop of whipped cream.

APPLESAUCE CRISP

APRICOT SCHAUM TORTELETS

BLUEBERRY COBBLERETTES

ORANGE CREPES

BLUEBERRY DOLLAR CAKES

STRAWBERRY BRUSCHETTA

CHOCOLATE-DIPPED CHERRIES

FRESH RASPBERRY SHOOTERS

Fruit and Berry Desserts

This chapter is filled with small versions of old-fashioned, homey desserts. Best of all, most of them can be made ahead. Serve what you need and freeze the rest for another day.

APPLESAUCE CRISP

Freshly made applesauce from flavorful, tart apples is, of course, the very best for this dessert, although you can use a good-quality commercially produced (nonsweetened) applesauce as well. Use little ramekins, about 1 ounce each, for these bite-size treats.

MAKES 12 (2-OUNCE) OR 24 (1-OUNCE) SERVINGS

2 cups applesauce
1 tablespoon fresh lemon juice
½ cup tightly packed brown sugar
½ teaspoon cinnamon

Crisp Topping (recipe follows)

Whipped cream (optional, for serving)

Preheat the oven to 375°F. Coat 12 shallow 2-ounce or 24 (1-ounce) baking dishes or ramekins with nonstick spray. Combine the applesauce, lemon juice, brown sugar, and cinnamon. Divide the mixture between the baking dishes.

Crisp Topping:

1 cup all-purpose flour
½ cup old-fashioned rolled oats
½ cup sugar
½ cup cold butter, cut up

For the topping, blend the flour, rolled oats, granulated sugar, and butter until crumbly. Sprinkle the mixture evenly over the applesauce.

Bake for 20–25 minutes until topping is lightly browned. Serve with whipped cream if desired.

APRICOT SCHAUM TORTELETS

These are pretty little desserts that look difficult to make, but really require just basic skills and very few ingredients. You can make these meringues any time you collect ½ cup of egg whites (which amounts to 4 egg whites). Since meringues are baked until completely dry, they can be stored in an airtight container in a cool place for a long time — even up to half a year. The filling is a delicious apricot jam, also easy to make any time of year, because you use dried apricots.

MAKES 48

4 large egg whites, at room temperature
¼ teaspoon salt
2 teaspoons cider or white vinegar
1 teaspoon pure vanilla extract
1 cup sugar
4 teaspoons cornstarch
Powdered sugar

Apricot Filling (recipe follows)

Lightly sweetened whipped cream (for topping)
Chopped pistachios (for garnish)

Preheat the oven to 200°F. Line two rimless baking sheets with parchment paper.

In a large bowl, with an electric mixer beat the egg whites and salt together until soft peaks form. Beat in the vinegar and vanilla. Stir the granulated sugar and cornstarch together in a separate bowl, then gradually add to the egg whites, beating until stiff and glossy, and the mixture holds stiff peaks, about 10 minutes at high speed.

continues

Drop meringues onto the parchment-covered baking sheets to make 2-inch "cookies." Put the powdered sugar into a small bowl. Dip your thumb into the powdered sugar, and then press down the center of each meringue cookie to make a slight indentation. Bake for 3–4 hours until the meringues are totally dry.

Apricot Filling:

1 cup (packed) dried apricots
1 cup water
1 cup sugar
2 tablespoons fresh lemon juice
½ teaspoon pure almond extract

In a large microwave-safe bowl, stir together the apricots, water, and sugar. Place into the microwave oven and cook at high speed for 10 minutes, or until the apricots are soft and puffed and have absorbed almost all of the liquid. Turn into the work bowl of a food processor with the steel blade in place and process until smooth, scraping the bowl as needed. Turn into a mixing bowl and add the lemon juice and almond extract. Stir to combine and set aside until needed. (This makes a wonderful apricot jam that can be made in advance and refrigerated in a covered container until needed.)

To serve tortelets, top meringues with a dollop of Apricot Filling and a dollop of whipped cream. Garnish with a few chopped pistachios.

BLUEBERRY COBBLERETTES

This is so easy to make, and the mini biscuits are similar to puffy little clouds. For these tiny desserts you will need small dishes or ramekins that hold 1 ounce each.

MAKES 12

½ cup sugar
1 tablespoon cornstarch
⅓ cup water
2 cups fresh blueberries
1 teaspoon butter (plus additional melted butter for pans)

Biscuits (recipe follows)

Whipped cream or cream to pour over (optional)

In a saucepan, combine the sugar, cornstarch, and water. Heat to a boil and add the blueberries. Bring to a boil again, then boil 1 minute, stirring, until thickened. Remove from the heat, add the 1 teaspoon butter, and set aside.

Brush 12 (1-ounce) baking dishes or ramekins with the additional melted butter. Place on a baking pan or baking sheet for easier handling. Divide the blueberry mixture evenly between the ramekins. (Ramekins can be covered and refrigerated for baking later at this point, if desired.)

Preheat the oven to 425°F.

continues

Biscuits:

1 cup all-purpose flour

1 tablespoon sugar

1½ teaspoons baking powder

¼ teaspoon salt

⅓ cup milk

4 tablespoons (½ stick) butter, melted

For the biscuits, in a bowl, stir together the flour, sugar, baking powder, and salt. Mix the milk and the melted butter and stir into the flour mixture just until moistened. On a floured surface, pat the dough out to about 1-inch thickness, dusting with additional flour if necessary. Using a 1½-inch-round cookie cutter or glass, cut out 12 biscuits. Place one on top of each of the blueberry-filled ramekins. Bake for 12–14 minutes or until the topping is lightly browned and the filling is bubbly. Serve warm with whipped cream if desired.

ORANGE CREPES

This is a version of Crepes Suzette, a favorite dessert made with thin pancakes soaked in an orange-flavored syrup and flamed before serving. Here you can opt to flame the dessert or not. If you don't have a crepe pan, an 8- or 9-inch omelet pan works well.

MAKES 12 SERVINGS OF 3 CREPES EACH

Crepes:
1 cup milk
2 tablespoons butter, melted
2 large eggs
1 cup all-purpose flour
¼ teaspoon salt
2 tablespoons sugar
Canola oil for cooking

Orange Syrup (recipe follows)

⅓ cup orange-flavored liqueur such as Cointreau or Grand Marnier (optional)
Powdered sugar (optional, for garnish)

For the crepes, in a medium-sized bowl, whisk together the milk, butter, and eggs. Whisk in the flour, salt, and sugar until smooth (this much you can do in a blender if desired). Let sit in the refrigerator for at least 1 hour or overnight.

Brush a crepe pan with oil and place over medium-high heat. Pour about 1 tablespoon of the batter into the pan and swirl around to make a 3-inch crepe. Cook until crepe begins to look dry, about 1 minute. Gently turn over the crepe in the pan and cook the other side, about 15 seconds. Transfer crepe onto a plate and continue cooking more crepes, brushing or wiping the pan with oil between each if necessary to prevent sticking.

continues

Orange Syrup:

4 tablespoons (½ stick) butter

3 tablespoons sugar

2 teaspoons grated orange zest

¼ cup fresh orange juice

For the syrup, in a skillet, melt the butter and add the sugar, orange zest, and juice. Heat to simmering. Fold each crepe in half and place them into the sauce. Using tongs or a spatula, fold crepes in half again to make a triangular shape. Work quickly so that all of the sauce is not absorbed by the first crepes. Place 3 crepes per serving onto a dessert dish.

Warm the liqueur and ignite, if desired. Pour over the crepes. Dust with powdered sugar if desired and serve immediately.

BLUEBERRY DOLLAR CAKES

*A favorite with kids, these pancakes make an appealing and quick-to-make dessert.
They are the very best with tiny wild blueberries, but if that is not possible,
cultivated blueberries will have to do!*

MAKES ABOUT 20

1 cup all-purpose flour
1 teaspoon baking powder
½ teaspoon salt
3 tablespoons sugar
1 large egg, separated
1 cup milk
2 tablespoons butter, melted
Fresh blueberries
Whipped cream (for serving)

In a medium mixing bowl, stir the flour, baking powder, salt, and sugar together. In another bowl, beat the egg yolk, milk, and melted butter. Stir the liquid mixture into the dry ingredients until blended. Beat the egg white until stiff and fold into the batter.

Heat a skillet or electric frying pan until a drop of water bounces when dripped onto the surface. Brush pan with oil.

Spoon about 2 tablespoons batter at a time into the pan. Drop 3 or 4 blueberries onto each pancake. Cook until pancake bubbles and the edge of the pancake is browned. Flip pancake over and brown on the other side.

Serve hot with more fresh blueberries and whipped cream.

STRAWBERRY BRUSCHETTA

The idea here is to make rusks out of sponge cake (see recipe on page 27). The rusks keep well once made. Top with a single big strawberry, and glaze with strawberry jelly.

MAKES 36

Sponge Cake (recipe page 27) (1 recipe will make almost 100 rusks)
Creamy Filling (recipe follows)
Strawberry Topping (recipe follows)

Prepare the Sponge Cake. Invert cake onto a work surface and with a sharp knife, cut it into 2-inch squares or into rounds about 2 inches in diameter. Split the pieces horizontally. Place on baking sheets. Heat the oven to 300°F. Bake for 10–15 minutes or until they have become dry and crisp rusks. Store in an airtight container until ready to serve.

Creamy Filling:
1 (3-ounce) package cream cheese
4 tablespoons (½ stick) butter, softened
1 cup powdered sugar
1 teaspoon pure vanilla extract

For the filling, in a small bowl, beat the cream cheese, butter, and sugar until smooth. Mix in the vanilla. Before serving, spread 36 rusks each with about ½ tablespoon of the Creamy Filling.

Strawberry Topping:
1 cup strawberry jelly
36 whole strawberries, cleaned and stemmed

For the topping, heat the jelly until liquid. Dip the strawberries into the jelly and place one on top of each cream-covered rusk.

75

CHOCOLATE-DIPPED CHERRIES

These are great to use as a garnish or as a tiny dessert all by itself. You can use either dark Bing cherries or light Michigan cherries.

MAKES 24

6 ounces bittersweet (not unsweetened), semisweet, or white chocolate, chopped
1 tablespoon light corn syrup
24 large fresh cherries with stems

Line a baking sheet with waxed paper. Place chocolate and corn syrup in a medium bowl and set over barely simmering water (do not allow bottom of pan to touch water); stir until melted and smooth.

Remove chocolate from over the water. Holding a cherry by its stem, dip it halfway into chocolate. Place the cherry, chocolate side down, on the waxed paper. Repeat with remaining cherries and chocolate. Chill until chocolate is firm, at least 15 minutes.

To serve, set cherries into small paper bonbon cups, or simply on a serving tray.

FRESH RASPBERRY SHOOTERS

So pretty, simple, and delicious, raspberries in a spicy white wine add color as well as lightness to a selection of mini desserts. Collect and chill your prettiest shot glasses; chill a bottle of sweet, spicy Gewürztraminer; and pick the plumpest red raspberries. You're set.

Per serving:

3 or 4 ripe, red raspberries
3–4 tablespoons chilled Gewürztraminer, sparkling apple juice, or Champagne
Sprig of fresh mint for garnish (optional)

Drop raspberries into 2- or 3-ounce chilled shot glasses. Pour wine over to cover the berries and garnish with a sprig of fresh mint.

CREAMY PUMPKIN MINI MOUSSES

PANNA COTTA THREE WAYS

ORANGE AND GINGER PANNA COTTA

CHOCOLATE ESPRESSO MOUSSE

CALLIOPE COFFEE

MANGO MOUSSE

WHITE CHOCOLATE MOUSSE

Mousses and Chilled Desserts

These are desserts that can, and must, be made ahead of time. Mousses can be refrigerated up to 4 or 5 days or even frozen, but the desserts that include gelatin (the panna cottas and the calliope coffee) do not freeze well. To freeze mousses for more than a few days, wrap them in plastic wrap (cups and all) and place into an airtight container. You can use plasticware (such as Tupperware) or tins that have covers to prevent them from being crushed. The freezer needs to be about 20°F or colder. Mousses can be kept frozen up to a month in most home freezers.

CREAMY PUMPKIN MINI MOUSSES

If you are trying to think of something different for dessert at Thanksgiving, here's an idea. Yummy, creamy, and spicy, these little mousses are perfect for any autumn meal. Besides that, they don't require baking, although they do require at least a few hours of chilling.

MAKES 20 (2-OUNCE) SERVINGS

1½ cups powdered sugar
1 (8-ounce) package cream cheese, softened
2 tablespoons butter, softened
1 tablespoon pure vanilla extract
1½ teaspoons pumpkin pie spice*
1 (15-ounce) can pumpkin puree
½ cup whipping cream, whipped
Whipped cream and finely chopped toasted pecans (for garnish)

In a mixing bowl, combine the powdered sugar, cream cheese, butter, vanilla extract, and spice. Beat with a hand mixer until light and fluffy. Add the pumpkin puree and mix until blended. Fold in the whipped cream.

Divide the mixture between 24 (2-ounce) ramekins, cups, or shot glasses. Chill 4 hours to overnight. Top with a small dollop of whipped cream and a sprinkle of toasted pecans before serving.

*If you don't have pumpkin pie spice, substitute 1 teaspoon ground cinnamon, ¼ teaspoon ground nutmeg, ⅛ teaspoon ground ginger, and ⅛ teaspoon ground cloves.

PANNA COTTA THREE WAYS

Panna Cotta is a traditional Italian dessert that translates to "cooked cream." This is a basic recipe with very simple variations for different flavors. I suggest serving a variety of flavors at one time — each one just a bite.

MAKES 12 (2-OUNCE) SERVINGS

Vanilla Panna Cotta:

3 cups whipping cream
1 package (1 tablespoon) unflavored gelatin
½ cup sugar
1–3 teaspoons pure vanilla extract (or flavoring from variations below)

Pour 1 cup of the cream into a medium saucepan and sprinkle the gelatin over the cream. Place over low heat and stir until gelatin has dissolved, about 5 minutes. Add the remaining cream and the sugar and stir until the sugar dissolves. Remove from heat.

If you decide to make 3 different flavors, divide the mixture into 3 portions, about 1 cup each. If you make all vanilla desserts, add 3 teaspoons vanilla to the entire cream mixture.

Coat 12 (2-ounce) ramekins with cooking spray. Pour mixture into the ramekins, dividing equally. You will have 12 total desserts. If you make 3 different flavors, you will have 4 desserts of each flavor.

Chill for 4 hours or overnight until desserts are set.

Serve in ramekins or remove to serving plates.

continues

VARIATIONS:

Chai Panna Cotta:

Bring ¼ cup milk to a boil and add 4 chai tea bags. Steep for 10 minutes. Remove the tea bags and squeeze liquid out of them. Discard tea bags. Add the remaining liquid to 1 (1-cup) portion of the cream mixture. Continue as directed in the basic recipe.

Milk Chocolate Panna Cotta:

Return 1 cup of the cream mixture to a saucepan. Mix in 4 ounces (chopped) milk chocolate. Place over low heat and stir until chocolate is melted and mixture is smooth. Continue as directed in the basic recipe.

ORANGE AND GINGER PANNA COTTA

Panna Cotta is one of the easiest desserts to make, and because this version is made in very tiny servings, you can be experimental with flavors. The combination of orange and ginger is exotic.

MAKES 12 (1-OUNCE) SERVINGS

1 package (1 tablespoon) unflavored gelatin
½ cup freshly squeezed orange juice
1½ cups heavy cream
3 tablespoons finely diced fresh gingerroot
⅓ cup sugar
1 tablespoon freshly grated orange zest
2 teaspoons pure vanilla extract
Shaved chocolate and orange segments (for garnish)

Sprinkle gelatin over 3 tablespoons orange juice and let it stand for about 10 minutes without stirring to soften the gelatin.

In a saucepan, combine cream and diced ginger. Cook over medium heat, stirring often, for 5 minutes until the cream is infused with ginger flavor. Add the sugar, orange zest, vanilla, and the remainder of the orange juice. Continue cooking over medium heat, stirring constantly to dissolve the sugar. Taste and add more sugar if needed.

When the cream mixture is heated through and starts simmering, remove from the heat. Add the softened gelatin and stir well to combine. Make sure the gelatin is completely dissolved.

Pour the cooked cream mixture through a fine sieve to remove the diced ginger and orange zest.

Divide the mixture between 12 (1-ounce) ramekins or small dessert molds. Chill for about 3 hours or overnight. To serve, remove desserts from the molds and garnish with shaved chocolate and orange segments.

CHOCOLATE ESPRESSO MOUSSE

For these rich mini mousses, glass or ceramic shot glasses work well. Chocolate-covered coffee beans are sold in coffee shops or in the coffee section of the supermarket. Remember to locate demitasse or similar little spoons for serving.

MAKES 12 (1-OUNCE) SERVINGS

3 tablespoons brewed coffee
3 tablespoons instant espresso coffee powder
1 cup whipping cream
4 ounces bittersweet chocolate, broken up
3 tablespoons superfine sugar
1 teaspoon pure vanilla extract
12 chocolate-covered coffee beans (for garnish)

In a small saucepan, or in a microwave-safe bowl, combine the brewed coffee and instant espresso powder. Stir in the cream. Place over medium-high heat until the cream is hot, or microwave uncovered, on high for 2 minutes or until cream is hot. Add the chocolate and sugar and stir until chocolate is melted. Stir in the vanilla. Pour into 12 (1-ounce) shot glasses or small dishes. Chill for 3 hours or until firm. Garnish each dessert with a chocolate-covered coffee bean.

CALLIOPE COFFEE

You have to love espresso coffee to love this dessert. In the heat of the summer, espresso, mixed with gelatin and chilled, makes an appealing miniature dessert. A calliope is a musical steam whistle that sits atop excursion boats that travel to the Mississippi River. The whistle was sounded to announce the boats arrival. The river boats still have a calliope today, but they don't serve the dessert anymore. Use little 1½-to 2-ounce metal cups, for easy removal, to shape this little treat. Tiny stemmed glasses are a perfect vehicle for serving this dessert.

MAKES APPROXIMATELY 12 SERVINGS

1 package (1 tablespoon) unflavored gelatin
¼ cup strong, cold espresso coffee
1½ cups hot espresso coffee
2 tablespoons sugar
Sweetened whipped cream (for topping)

Soften the gelatin in the cold espresso. Stir in the hot espresso and sugar, and stir until gelatin and sugar are dissolved. Cool to room temperature. Pour into 12 small cups. Cover and chill until set.

To remove desserts from the molds, dip quickly in warm water then turn out onto serving plates or into glasses. Top with sweetened whipped cream.

꙳

MANGO MOUSSE

Mango adds creaminess and a tropical flavor to this rich little dessert spiked by the tartness of buttermilk. These minimousses are pretty served in stemmed glasses. If you don't have a dozen matching dishes, don't worry — the variety only adds to the presentation.

MAKES 12 (2-OUNCE) SERVINGS

1 package (1 tablespoon) unflavored gelatin
2 tablespoons cold water
1 cup whipping cream
½ cup half-and-half
½ cup low-fat buttermilk
½ cup sugar
¼ cup strained mango pulp*
1 tablespoon pure vanilla extract
Diced fresh mango and/or chopped pistachios (for garnish)

Coat 12 (2-ounce) ramekins with cooking spray.

In a small dish, sprinkle the gelatin over the cold water. In a saucepan, heat the cream, half-and-half, buttermilk, sugar, and mango pulp. Heat just to a simmer. Remove from the heat and stir in the gelatin and vanilla until blended and gelatin is totally dissolved.

Divide the mixture between the prepared ramekins. Cover and chill for at least 4–5 hours.

To serve, run a thin-tipped knife around the edge of the ramekins and turn the mousse out onto a serving plate. Top with diced mango and/or chopped pistachios.

* To strain the mango pulp, peel and pit the mango; cut into cubes. In a food processor or blender, puree the mango until smooth; pour into a strainer and press into a measuring cup.

WHITE CHOCOLATE MOUSSE

For this dessert you will need 12 shot glasses or demitasse cups that each hold 1 ounce (2 tablespoons). Or, you can buy chocolate cordial cups in various sizes that hold anywhere from ½ ounce to 1 ounce each. These are fun because you can just pop the whole thing into your mouth. For the best flavor, be sure to use a good-quality imported white chocolate.

MAKES 12 (1-OUNCE) SERVINGS

4 ounces white chocolate, broken up
¼ cup whole milk
2 tablespoons light corn syrup
½ cup whipping cream
Toasted slivered almonds or fresh raspberries (for garnish)

In a small saucepan or a microwave-safe bowl, combine the white chocolate and milk. Place saucepan over medium heat or put the microwave-safe bowl, uncovered, in the microwave oven on high. Stirring often, heat until milk is hot and chocolate is melted. Cool to lukewarm. Stir in the corn syrup.

Whip the cream and fold into the cooled mixture. Divide the mixture between cups or glasses, depending on the size of the containers. Cover and refrigerate for about 4 hours until firm. Can be prepared 2–3 days before serving.

Garnish with toasted slivered almonds or fresh raspberries before serving.

RICOTTA CRANBERRY CUSTARDS

COCONUT RICE PUDDINGS

PUMPKIN CREAM POTS

CHOCOLATE SOUFFLÉS

MINIATURE BREAD PUDDINGS

CLASSIC CRÈME BRÛLÉE

RHUBARB CRÈME BRÛLÉE

HAZELNUT CRÈME BRÛLÉE

VANILLA POTS DE CRÈME

MOCHA RUM POTS DE CRÈME

FRESH GINGER ICE CREAM

FROZEN MAPLE FRANGO

Creams, Custards, and Frozen Desserts

Many of these egg-based desserts are quite rich, but don't need to
be eliminated from your menu for that reason. They're perfect for
miniature servings since just a bite satisfies the desire for dessert.
Frozen desserts like the Maple Frango and the ice creams offer
wonderful flavors with temperature contrast.

RICOTTA CRANBERRY CUSTARDS

Almost cheesecakes, these custards are balanced with a fresh cranberry sauce.

MAKES 24 (2-OUNCE) SERVINGS

12 ounces (1½ 8-ounce packages) cream cheese, at room temperature
¾ cup ricotta cheese
2 large eggs
½ teaspoon pure vanilla extract
½ cup sugar
½ cup heavy cream

Cranberry Sauce (recipe follows)

Preheat the oven to 250°F. Have available 20–24 (2-ounce) ramekins. Adjust oven rack to center position.

In a large bowl, using an electric mixer on medium speed, beat the cream cheese until light and fluffy, about 2 minutes. Add the ricotta and mix until blended. Add the eggs, 1 at a time, mixing after each addition until completely incorporated. Add the vanilla, sugar, and cream and mix until combined.

Spoon the batter among the ramekins dividing equally. Place ramekins in a large, rimmed baking dish and place on the oven rack. Pour enough hot water into the baking pan around the ramekins to reach about halfway up the sides. Bake for 30–45 minutes, until set. The top should not have changed color at all. Remove from the oven and from the water bath. Set aside to cool slightly, then refrigerate until chilled through, about 3 hours.

continues

Cranberry Sauce:

2 cups fresh or frozen cranberries
1 cup water
1 cup sugar

Place the cranberries, water, and sugar in a saucepan over medium-high heat and bring to a boil. The skins of the cranberries should all burst within a minute. Remove from the heat, set aside to cool slightly, then cover and refrigerate until chilled through, at least 3 hours. Serve chilled, spooned over the ricotta custards.

COCONUT RICE PUDDINGS

This is a simple baked rice custard with a delicate coconut flavor.

MAKES 12 (2-OUNCE) SERVINGS

Melted butter and granulated sugar for ramekins
¾ cup cooked rice (grain length unimportant)
3 large eggs, lightly beaten
¼ cup sugar
1 (13.5-ounce) can unsweetened coconut milk
½ cup light cream or half-and-half
1 teaspoon pure vanilla extract
⅓ cup sweetened flaked coconut
Toasted coconut (for serving)

Preheat the oven to 275°F. Brush 12 (2-ounce) ramekins with melted butter and dust with granulated sugar. Adjust oven rack to center position.

Mix the rice, eggs, sugar, coconut milk, half-and-half, vanilla, and coconut until well blended. Pour into the prepared ramekins, dividing mixture equally.

Place ramekins in a rimmed baking dish. Place into the oven and add hot water to the pan to come about halfway up the sides of the ramekins. Bake for 30–35 minutes or until puddings are set. Remove from the oven and cool. Sprinkle with the toasted coconut before serving.

PUMPKIN CREAM POTS

Pumpkin custard is baked in small ovenproof dishes, anywhere from 4-ounce ramekins to 2-ounce eggcups. For a fun alternative to a big slice of pumpkin pie, cut leaf shapes from pastry, either purchased or your own favorite recipe, and use to decorate the pots. Reroll scraps of pastry and cut sticks to use to dip into the creamy pumpkin dessert.

MAKES 8 (4-OUNCE) OR 16 (2-OUNCE) DESSERTS

1 (15-ounce) can pumpkin puree
3 large eggs
½ cup granulated sugar
½ cup packed light brown sugar
2 teaspoons pumpkin pie spice*
½ teaspoon salt
1 (12-ounce) can undiluted evaporated milk

Pie Crust Decorations (optional; instructions follow)

Preheat the oven to 350°F. Have available 8 (4-ounce) ramekins, or 16 (2-ounce) ovenproof dishes.

In a 2-quart bowl with a whisk, mix the pumpkin puree and eggs until combined. Add the granulated and brown sugars and mix until combined. Add the pumpkin pie spice, salt, and evaporated milk and mix until combined. Divide the pumpkin mixture equally among the dishes and bake until the top is dry and lightly browned and a knife inserted into the center comes out almost completely clean, 30–35 minutes for 4-ounce ramekins, 15–25 minutes for small cups. (The timing will vary dramatically according to the size and type of ramekin.) Set aside to cool slightly. Serve warm or cover and refrigerate overnight and serve chilled, garnished with pie crust decorations, if desired.

*If you do not have pumpkin pie spice mix, you can substitute 1 teaspoon ground cinnamon, ½ teaspoon ground ginger, ⅛ teaspoon ground nutmeg, and ⅛ teaspoon ground cloves.

continues

Pie Crust Decorations:

Pie pastry dough (favorite homemade pastry dough or thawed frozen pie dough)
Milk (for brushing)
Granulated sugar (for dusting)

Preheat oven to 375°F. On a floured surface, roll the pastry to a thickness of a little thinner than ¼ inch. Using a paring knife or small cookie cutter, cut out leaf shapes and place on a baking sheet. If desired, use the tip of the knife to draw the leaf spine on the dough, inserting the knife about halfway into the dough. Reroll the pastry scraps and cut into thin strips; twist and place on the baking sheet. Brush each leaf and stick lightly with a little milk and sprinkle with sugar. Bake for 8–10 minutes, until golden brown. Store in an airtight container.

Garnish each pot with pie crust leaves and serve with a pie crust stick.

CHOCOLATE SOUFFLÉS

These soufflés can be made and refrigerated (for up to 8 hours) or frozen (wrapped in foil) until you are ready to bake them. Add 5 minutes to baking time for frozen soufflés.

MAKES 12 (2-OUNCE) SOUFFLÉS

1 tablespoon cornstarch
¾ cup low-fat (2%) milk
⅓ cup superfine granulated sugar
4 (1-ounce) squares bittersweet chocolate
1 teaspoon pure vanilla extract
Melted butter and sugar for soufflé dishes
4 large egg whites, at room temperature
1 teaspoon lemon juice
Powdered sugar (for serving)

In a small saucepan, blend the cornstarch with the milk and half the sugar. Place over medium-high heat until mixture comes to a boil. Reduce heat to low and stir for 2 minutes. Remove from heat and stir in the chocolate and vanilla. Stir until chocolate is melted, then set mixture aside to cool to room temperature.

Preheat oven to 350°F. Butter and sprinkle with sugar 12 (2-ounce) ramekins or baking dishes.

Whip the egg whites with the lemon juice until foamy, then beat in the remaining sugar until the egg whites form stiff peaks.

Using a rubber spatula, fold the beaten whites into the chocolate mixture. Divide the mixture between the prepared baking dishes. Place them into a rimmed baking dish and add ½-inch of hot water to the baking dish. Bake for 20 minutes or until puffed and set. Remove from the oven and dust with powdered sugar before serving. The soufflés will collapse slightly.

MINIATURE BREAD PUDDINGS

You can bake a variety of flavors of bread pudding using this recipe. For starters, I sprinkle the baking cups with cinnamon sugar. Choose your favorite add-in from those listed below, or flavor all the bread puddings differently to mix it up.

MAKES 12 (2-OUNCE) SERVINGS

1½ cups half-and-half
½ cup light brown sugar
2 tablespoons butter
3 large eggs
1 tablespoon pure vanilla extract
3 cups cubed white bread, preferably French bread, no crusts
Melted butter, cinnamon sugar, brown sugar, or plain sugar for baking cups

Optional additions:
Raisins or diced fresh apple
Chocolate chips
Chopped pecans or walnuts
Berry jam

Caramel Drizzle (recipe page 32) or lightly whipped cream (for serving)

Preheat the oven to 350°F.

In a saucepan, combine the half-and-half, brown sugar, and butter. Bring to a boil and simmer just until the sugar is dissolved. Whisk eggs and vanilla extract together. Add the hot mixture, whisking constantly, until well blended. Add bread cubes.

Brush 12 (2-ounce) ramekins or baking cups with butter. Sprinkle with granulated sugar, brown sugar, or cinnamon sugar. Add raisins, diced apple, chocolate chips, chopped nuts, or jam to the cups (they don't have to all be the same).

continues

Spoon the bread pudding mixture into the prepared ramekins or baking cups, then set them in a shallow, rimmed baking dish. Place on center oven rack and add about ¼- to ½-inch of very hot water to the baking pan. Bake for 12–15 minutes, or until puddings are set.

Cool, and loosen edge of each pudding with a knife and turn out onto serving plates. Top with Caramel Drizzle or lightly whipped cream.

Classic Crème Brûlée

I cooked my first batch in tiny demitasse cups, filling them by half. Then, after calling around, I found 2-ounce metal cups from a restaurant supply store that cost only 49 cents each and they worked well, too. This is an easy recipe to put together. A regular blowtorch is handy for melting the sugar on top. Note that the baking time has a wide range, because it will vary with the size and type of dish used.

MAKES 12 (2-OUNCE) SERVINGS

2 cups heavy cream
5 large egg yolks
½ cup sugar, preferably superfine or baker's sugar
1 tablespoon pure vanilla extract
½ cup light brown sugar (approximate)

Preheat the oven to 275°F. Have available 12 small dessert ramekins or 2-ounce custard cups.

Whisk the cream and egg yolks together until perfectly blended. Put mixture through a fine strainer to remove little lumps from the egg yolks. Mix in the sugar and vanilla. Pour into the 12 cups and place in a large, rimmed baking dish. Pour about 1 inch of very hot water into the baking dish around the cups. Bake for 35–55 minutes, checking for doneness by inserting a knife into the center of one; if it comes out clean, they're done. Be careful not to overcook or, like a custard, the crèmes will separate.

Remove from the baking dish and set on a counter to cool. Chill at least 3 hours before serving.

To serve, spread a thin layer of brown sugar on top of each to cover completely. With a blowtorch, melt the layer of brown sugar until it caramelizes. (The sugar will melt and then harden.) You can do this under the broiler, but I have more luck with a blowtorch.

RHUBARB CRÈME BRÛLÉE

Rhubarb is a springtime favorite in many northern areas of the country. People either love it or they don't. The stalks are sour but very flavorful in desserts and juices. The leaves are toxic, as are the roots of the rhubarb. Sugar and cream in the crème brûlée soften and mellow the flavor of rhubarb to make a delicious dessert. This miniature dessert is a perfect way to introduce rhubarb to the novice.

MAKES 12 (2-OUNCE) SERVINGS

2 cups rhubarb, cut in ½ inch pieces
6 teaspoons sugar
5 large egg yolks
½ cup sugar
2 cups heavy cream
1 teaspoon pure vanilla extract
½ cup brown sugar (approximate)

Preheat the oven to 350°F. Coat a 9 x 13-inch glass baking dish with cooking spray. Arrange rhubarb in an even layer in the baking dish and bake for 30–40 minutes or until the rhubarb is tender and the liquid has evaporated. Remove from the oven.

Reduce oven temperature to 325°F. Scoop the rhubarb into 12 (2-ounce) ovenproof ramekins or custard cups. Sprinkle each with ½ teaspoon sugar.

In a bowl, whisk the egg yolks, ½ cup sugar, cream, and vanilla together. Pour the cream mixture over the rhubarb, dividing the mixture equally.

Place filled ramekins into a larger rimmed baking dish and add enough hot water to reach halfway up the sides of the ramekins. Bake until set, about 25–30 minutes.

Remove baking dish from oven, then remove ramekins to cool on a rack.

continues

Just before serving, sprinkle 1 tablespoon brown sugar evenly over each custard. Make sure the sugar completely covers the custard. With a blowtorch, melt the layer of brown sugar until it caramelizes. (The sugar will melt and then harden.) You can do this step under the broiler (2–3 minutes), but I have more luck with a blowtorch.

Hazelnut Crème Brûlée

Shallow ramekins are ideal for this classic dessert. Each serving is about ¼ of the classic size.

MAKES 12 (2-OUNCE) SERVINGS

2 cups heavy cream
5 large egg yolks
½ cup sugar
1 tablespoon pure vanilla extract
¼ cup chopped toasted hazelnuts
½ cup light brown sugar (approximate)

Preheat oven to 275°F. Have available 12 small dessert ramekins or 2-ounce custard cups.

Whisk the cream, egg yolks, sugar, and vanilla extract together in a bowl until the mixture is nice and creamy. Divide the toasted hazelnuts between the 12 ramekins. Pour the creamy mixture through a fine strainer onto the hazelnuts, dividing mixture evenly.

Place filled ramekins in a rimmed baking dish and place in the oven. Add hot water to the dish until it comes about halfway up the sides of the ramekins. Bake for 30–35 minutes until custard is set. Check for doneness every 10 minutes. You'll know they're done when you can stick a knife in one and it comes out clean. Remove the baking dish from the oven and remove individual ramekins from the water. Set them on the counter, and let cool for 15 minutes. Refrigerate 8 hours or overnight.

Just before serving, sprinkle a thin layer of the light brown sugar on the top of each. Make sure it completely covers the custard. With a blowtorch, melt the layer of brown sugar until it caramelizes. (The sugar will melt and then harden.) You can do this step under the broiler, but I have more luck with a blowtorch.

VANILLA POTS DE CRÈME

The most famous cream-based liqueur is one that is made by R.A. Bailey & Co. of Dublin, Ireland. There are similar liqueurs on the market that can be used in this rich dessert. If you prefer not to have an alcoholic ingredient, substitute flavored dairy half-and-half.

MAKES 15

1½ cups heavy cream
1 cup milk
1 cup Bailey's Irish Cream, vanilla cream liqueur, or flavored dairy half-and-half
8 large egg yolks
½ cup sugar
Pinch of salt
1 teaspoon pure vanilla extract

Preheat the oven to 325°F. Set 15 demitasse cups or 3- to 4-ounce pots de crème cups into a large rimmed baking dish.

Combine 1 cup of the cream and the milk in a heavy saucepan or microwave-safe dish. Heat to boiling.

In a large bowl, whisk the liqueur, egg yolks, sugar, salt, and vanilla until blended. Whisk in the hot milk mixture until smooth. Pour mixture through a fine sieve into a 4-cup measure.

Pour the mixture into the demitasse cups or pot de crème cups, dividing the mixture evenly. Place the rimmed baking dish on the center rack of the oven, and pour very hot water into the baking dish to come about halfway up the sides of the filled cups.

continues

Bake for 20–22 minutes until just set in the centers. Do not overbake. Remove from the oven and carefully remove cups from the water. Allow to cool, cover with plastic wrap, and chill at least 4 hours or overnight.

To serve, beat the remaining ½ cup heavy cream until soft peaks form. Spoon cream into a pastry bag with a star-shaped tip. Pipe a star into the middle of each dish and serve.

MOCHA RUM POTS DE CRÈME

These little custards are simple to make, yet rich and decadent. To lighten the custards, you can make them with milk, but for the full effect, try them at least once with cream.

MAKES 12 SERVINGS

2 cups heavy cream or milk
½ cup milk
2 squares bittersweet chocolate
1 tablespoon instant espresso coffee powder
1 tablespoon dark rum
6 large egg yolks
¼ cup sugar
2 teaspoons pure vanilla extract
Whipped cream (for garnish)

Preheat the oven to 325°F. Adjust oven rack to center position. Select 12 small (4- to 5-ounce) demitasse cups or little ovenproof ramekins.

In a saucepan, combine the heavy cream, milk, and chocolate; place over medium-low heat until chocolate is melted, stirring occasionally. Dissolve the espresso powder in the dark rum and whisk into the cream after the chocolate has melted.

Whisk the egg yolks, sugar, and vanilla together in a small bowl. Whisk ¼ of the hot cream mixture into the egg mixture; mix well. Whisk the entire egg mixture into the remaining cream mixture until well blended.

Pour mixture through a fine-mesh strainer into a measuring cup. Divide the mixture equally between the baking cups. Place cups into a large, square rimmed baking dish. Put the baking dish

continues

in the oven and pour hot water into the dish to come halfway up the sides of the cups.

Bake for 25–30 minutes until custards are set but still jiggly. Remove from the oven, remove cups from the hot water bath, and cool. Cover and chill until ready to serve.

Just before serving, put whipped cream into a pastry bag and press out little dollops of cream around the edges of the desserts.

FRESH GINGER ICE CREAM

Who can resist a little dab of ultra-rich ice cream? If you have an electric ice cream maker, this is really simple, but I have a soft spot in my heart for the old-fashioned ice and rock salt churn. Of course, either works here. Serve little scoops in aperitif or shot glasses.

MAKES ABOUT 1 QUART

4 cups half-and-half or half cream, half milk
1 (1-inch) piece fresh gingerroot, peeled, chopped
⅔ cup sugar
2 large egg yolks, lightly beaten
1 tablespoon cornstarch

Combine 1 cup of the half-and-half with the chopped ginger in a medium saucepan. Bring to a boil. Remove from heat, cover, and let stand 30 minutes. Pour mixture into the container of an electric blender. Top with the cover and process until the gingerroot is crushed. Strain, discarding the gingerroot pieces. Set strained mixture aside.

Combine the second cup of half-and-half with the sugar, egg yolks, and cornstarch. Cook over low heat, stirring, until mixture is slightly thickened. Remove from the heat and set aside to cool. Mix the ginger-flavored cream with the thickened egg-cream and the remaining 2 cups half-and-half. Cover and chill 1–2 hours.

Pour mixture into the freezer can of a 1-gallon hand-turned or electric 2-quart ice cream maker. Freeze according to manufacturer's instructions. Scoop ice cream into small dishes or shot glasses and serve immediately.

FROZEN MAPLE FRANGO

Dating back to 1918, Frozen Frango was the name of a dessert sold in a fancy tearoom in Seattle. The first frango reportedly was maple-flavored, although orange frango was also available. Frango is very easy to make and can be served like ice cream in small fluted glasses. Frango has a classic crystalline structure that is not icy, and a very smooth, rich texture. Be sure to use pure maple syrup to get the right flavor in this delicious dessert.

MAKES 12 (2-OUNCE) SERVINGS

¾ cup pure maple syrup
4 large egg yolks, beaten
2 cup whipping cream

Pour the maple syrup into a small, heavy saucepan and bring to a boil over medium-high heat. Beat the egg yolks in a small bowl. Whisk a small amount of the boiling syrup into the egg yolks, then whisk the mixture into the hot syrup. Cook, stirring constantly, until thickened.

Remove from the heat and cool to room temperature. Whip the cream until stiff, then fold the maple mixture into the whipped cream. Turn into an 8-inch square cake pan and freeze 4–6 hours (uncovered) or overnight (covered in plastic wrap).

Just before serving, scoop the frozen dessert into small glasses.

MINI CREAM PUFFS

ITALIAN RICOTTA AND FRUIT
FILLED CREAM PUFFS

CRISPY CREAM PUFFS

DULCE DE LECHE CREAM PUFFS

MINIATURE SWEDISH MARIA PASTRIES

GREEK-STYLE HONEY-NUT PASTRIES

CHOCOLATE HAZELNUT ÉCLAIRS

CHOCOLATE-DIPPED ALMOND BISCOTTI

COCONUT GINGER MACAROONS

NORWEGIAN CREAM CONES

Pastries and Sweets

From easy-to-make cream puffs to chewy macaroons, pastries
are especially good candidates for petite sweets. Filled pastries
are usually quite rich, but with these mini portions,
you can still enjoy your favorites.

MINI CREAM PUFFS

These mini cream puffs can be filled simply with whipped cream, with a vanilla custard, or with ice cream. They can also be frozen until you are ready to fill and serve them.

MAKES 24

1 cup water
8 tablespoons (1 stick) butter
½ teaspoon salt
1½ teaspoons sugar
1 cup all-purpose flour
4 large eggs

Preheat the oven to 425°F. Combine the water, butter, salt, and sugar in a large saucepan and bring to a rolling boil over medium-high heat. When it boils, immediately take the pan off the heat. Add all the flour at once and stir hard until all the flour is incorporated. Place over low heat and cook, stirring, about 2 minutes to evaporate some of the moisture.

Turn dough into a food processor with the steel blade in place. Turn the processor on and add the eggs, one at a time. Mix until totally incorporated and dough is glossy and smooth.

Line two baking sheets with parchment paper. Scoop the dough into small mounds about 1 to 1½ inches in diameter and place evenly onto the baking sheets.

Bake for 15 minutes, then reduce temperature to 375°F and bake until puffed, golden, and dry, about 25 minutes more. Allow to cool on the baking sheet.

ITALIAN RICOTTA AND FRUIT FILLED CREAM PUFFS

The filling for these cream puffs is reminiscent of the classic Italian dessert, cannoli.

MAKES 24

24 Mini Cream Puffs (recipe page 124)

Ricotta and Fruit Filling:

1 cup whole milk ricotta cheese, drained*
½ cup powdered sugar
1 teaspoon pure vanilla extract
2 tablespoons semisweet mini chocolate chips
2 tablespoons finely chopped candied citrus peel
¼ cup heavy cream, whipped
Powdered sugar (for garnish)

Slice the tops off the baked and cooled cream puffs.

For the filling, mix the ricotta, powdered sugar, vanilla, chocolate chips, and candied fruit together. Fold in the whipped cream.

Spoon about 1 tablespoon of the filling into each cream puff and place tops back onto the puffs. Refrigerate until ready to serve. Lightly dust with powdered sugar before serving.

*To drain, turn the ricotta into a sieve over a bowl. Allow to drain at least 2 hours.

CRISPY CREAM PUFFS

Fashioned after the flavors of the famous doughnuts, these crispy little cream puffs have a glaze and a frosting to finish them off. The flavor is the best if you glaze, frost, and eat the cream puffs just after baking.

MAKES 24

24 Mini Cream Puffs (recipe page 124)

Cream Glaze:
5 tablespoons butter
2 cups powdered sugar
1½ teaspoons pure vanilla extract
4–6 tablespoons hot water
½ cup milk chocolate chips, melted
1–2 tablespoons chocolate sprinkles (for garnish)

While the Mini Cream Puffs are baking, prepare the glaze. Mix the butter, powdered sugar, vanilla, and enough hot water to make a smooth glaze. Turn half of the glaze into another bowl and mix in the melted chocolate chips.

Dip the freshly baked cream puffs first into the plain creamy glaze. Put the puffs on a rack and when the glaze has set, dip into the chocolate glaze. Sprinkle with chocolate sprinkles while still sticky and put aside until glazes are set.

DULCE DE LECHE CREAM PUFFS

Dulce de Leche is the favorite caramel sauce of South America. You can make the little cream puffs ahead and freeze them until you are ready to serve. In fact, you can fill the puffs with the ice cream and then freeze them for up to a week ahead of serving. The caramel sauce goes on just before serving.

MAKES 24

24 Mini Cream Puffs (recipe page 124)

Dulce de Leche Sauce:
20 milk caramels
½ cup heavy cream

1 pint vanilla or caramel-flavored ice cream

Slice the tops off the baked and cooled cream puffs.

For the Dulce de Leche Sauce, combine the caramels and heavy cream in a microwave-safe bowl. Microwave at high power 30 seconds at a time, until caramel is melted into a sauce.

Shape small scoops of ice cream and place into the cream puffs. Replace the tops and drizzle with sauce and serve.

MINIATURE SWEDISH MARIA PASTRIES

Although this recipe looks complicated, it is made up of four simple steps. These delicious pastries have a base of butter pastry, which is cut into small rounds and then topped with choux paste and baked. The puffs are filled with a cream filling and either frosted with powdered sugar icing or simply dusted with powdered sugar.

MAKES ABOUT 60

Butter Pastry:

1 cup all-purpose flour
6 tablespoons firm butter, cut up
2–3 tablespoons ice water

Preheat the oven to 400°F. Cover baking sheets with parchment paper.

For the pastry, measure the flour into the work bowl of a food processor with the steel blade in place. Add the butter and process using on/off pulses until the butter is the size of peas. Turn into a mixing bowl. Add the ice water and toss until a dough forms. Press into a ball and roll dough out to about ¼-inch thickness. Cut small rounds, 1½ inches in diameter. Place them about 2 inches apart on baking sheets.

Choux Paste:

1 cup water
8 tablespoons (1 stick) butter
1 tablespoon sugar
¼ teaspoon salt
1 cup all-purpose flour
3 large eggs

For the Choux Paste, measure the water into a heavy, small saucepan. Place over high heat and add the butter; bring to a boil. Stir until butter is melted. Add the sugar, salt, and flour, and

continues

129

stir until mixture is stiff and comes away from the sides of the pan. Remove from heat and add the eggs one at a time, beating after each addition until dough is very smooth and glossy. Cool to room temperature. Pipe each pastry round with about a tablespoonful of the Choux Paste. Bake for 20–25 minutes until puffed and golden. Cool. The cooled pastries can be covered and refrigerated for up to 2 days before filling.

Cream Filling:

1 cup light cream
2 large egg yolks
¼ cup sugar
1 tablespoon cornstarch
1 teaspoon unflavored gelatin
1 teaspoon pure vanilla extract
1 cup whipping cream, whipped

For the Cream Filling, combine the light cream, egg yolks, sugar, cornstarch, and gelatin in a heavy saucepan. Heat, stirring, until mixture comes to a boil and thickens. Cool to room temperature. Cover and chill. Before using the filling, fold in the vanilla and whipped cream.

Frosting:

1 cup powdered sugar
2 tablespoons softened butter
2–3 tablespoons milk
1 teaspoon pure almond extract

To finish, make a slit near the base of the pastries and pipe in the Cream Filling. Mix the frosting ingredients together until smooth. Drizzle pastries with the frosting. Serve immediately or chill until ready to serve.

GREEK-STYLE HONEY-NUT PASTRIES

Phyllo (or filo) dough is available frozen in supermarkets everywhere. Using the paper-thin dough, Greeks make baklava, a honey pastry. Another pastry dough, not as easy to find, is called "kataifi" and looks like shredded wheat. To simulate kataifi, you shred phyllo dough with a sharp knife. These little pastries are easy to keep frozen and can be heated up as needed.

MAKES 24

1 package (1 pound) frozen phyllo dough, thawed
⅔ cup melted butter
1 cup coarsely chopped walnuts
1 teaspoon ground cinnamon
⅛ teaspoon ground cloves
1 tablespoon dry bread crumbs

Honey Syrup (recipe follows)

On a working surface, make a stack of 5 phyllo sheets, brushing each sheet with melted butter (use about half the butter). Cut the stack into 24 squares. Line the cavities of a 24-cup miniature muffin pan with the phyllo squares. Trim ends to form round cups. Cover with a damp cloth to keep the pastry moist.

Roll up the remaining pastry and, with a sharp knife, cut into very thin shreds (about ¹⁄₁₆-inch thick). Divide into 24 equal portions. Cover with a damp cloth and set aside.

Mix the walnuts, cinnamon, cloves, and bread crumbs in a bowl.

Take one portion of the shredded phyllo at a time and shape it into a small bird's nest. Put ½ tablespoonful of the nut mixture into the center of the "nest" and roll it up into a ball. Place into the center of a pastry-lined muffin cup. Repeat the process to fill the remaining muffin cups.

continues

Preheat the oven to 350°F. Brush pastry tops with the remaining butter. Bake pastries for 25–35 minutes until golden brown.

Honey Syrup:

1 cup sugar
1 cup water
1 cup honey
Peel from 1 lemon
1 tablespoon lemon juice

While pastries are baking, prepare the Honey Syrup: Bring all ingredients to a boil. Simmer for 10 minutes. Strain and cool slightly.

Drizzle baked pastries with the syrup. Serve warm or chilled, or freeze pastries until ready to serve.

CHOCOLATE HAZELNUT ÉCLAIRS

You can make the éclairs ahead of time and freeze them, unfilled, for several weeks, well-wrapped. The filling can be made up to 2 days ahead and kept chilled. Prepare the chocolate glaze on the day you assemble and serve the éclairs.

MAKES 36

Éclairs:
1 cup water
½ cup butter
1 cup all-purpose flour
4 large eggs

Chocolate Hazelnut Filling (recipe follows)

Chocolate Glaze: (recipe follows)

Crushed Amaretti cookies (optional for garnish)

Preheat the oven to 425°F. Cover a baking sheet with parchment paper.

In a saucepan, combine the water and butter. Place over high heat and bring to a boil, melting the butter. Add flour all at once and stir until mixture forms a ball, about 1 minute. Remove pan from heat and cool 5 minutes. Turn mixture into a food processor with the steel blade in place. With the motor going, add the eggs, one at a time, making a smooth mixture.

Put dough into a pastry bag and pipe into strips about the size of your index finger on the baking sheet. Bake for about 15 minutes or until puffed and golden. Remove to a rack to cool.

continues

Chocolate Hazelnut Filling:

1 cup whipping cream
½ cup chocolate hazelnut spread such as Nutella

In a large bowl, whip the cream until stiff and fold in the chocolate hazelnut spread. Chill for up to 2 days, if desired.

Chocolate Glaze:

6 tablespoons whipping cream
6 tablespoons light corn syrup
8 ounces semisweet chocolate, chopped

For the glaze, in a small heavy saucepan, combine the cream and corn syrup. Heat to boiling. Reduce heat to low. Add chocolate; whisk until smooth. Remove from heat. Let cool until glaze thickens slightly but can still be poured, about 25 minutes.

To assemble the éclairs, fill a pastry bag with the Chocolate Hazelnut Filling. Punch a hole in one end of each éclair and pipe the filling into the hole until you feel the pressure of cream against the sides of the pastry. Brush each éclair with the Chocolate Glaze and let dry. They may be kept at room temperature up to 2 hours or refrigerated up to 8 hours before serving.

VARIATION:

Peanut Butter–Chocolate Éclairs:
Follow recipe for Chocolate Hazelnut Éclairs, substituting good-quality peanut butter for the chocolate hazelnut spread in the filling.

CHOCOLATE-DIPPED ALMOND BISCOTTI

These are mini biscotti — 2½ to 3 inches long.

MAKES ABOUT 48

½ cup sugar
4 tablespoons (½ stick) butter, melted
1 teaspoon pure almond extract
½ cup almonds, chopped
2 large eggs, at room temperature
1¼ cups all-purpose flour
1½ teaspoons baking powder
¼ teaspoon salt
1 cup semisweet chocolate chips (for dipping)

Preheat the oven to 350°F. Cover a baking sheet with parchment paper.

In a large mixing bowl, using a hand mixer, cream the sugar and butter until smooth. Add the almond extract, almonds, and eggs and beat until smooth. Mix in the flour, baking powder, and salt. Divide the mixture into two parts, and on a floured board, shape each part into a 15-inch-long strand. Place the strands on the baking sheet about 4 inches apart.

Bake for 20–25 minutes or until firm. Remove from the oven and let cool slightly. When cool enough to handle, cut into ½-inch diagonal slices. Return to baking sheet. Bake for 15–25 minutes, turning once, until both sides are lightly browned and toasted.

Place chocolate chips into a small bowl. Set over just-simmering water until chips are melted. Dip one side of each biscotti into the melted chocolate and return to the paper-covered baking sheet until chocolate is set. Store in an airtight container.

COCONUT GINGER MACAROONS

These are so simple to make. Just be sure to drop the batter in very tiny mounds on the baking sheets. They are extra-special dipped in melted milk chocolate. The macaroons keep well. Pack them in airtight containers and store either in the freezer or a cool place.

MAKES ABOUT 48

2 large egg whites
1 (14-ounce) can sweetened condensed milk
¼ teaspoon salt
¼ cup finely chopped candied ginger
1 (14-ounce) bag sweetened flaked coconut (5⅓ cups)
1 cup milk chocolate chips (for dipping)

Preheat the oven to 325°F. Coat three rimless cookie sheets with cooking spray or cover with parchment paper.

In a mixing bowl with a wooden spoon, stir together the egg whites, sweetened condensed milk, salt, and candied ginger until well blended, about 1 minute.

Stir in the coconut, using a rubber spatula, until all the moist ingredients are thoroughly blended with the coconut.

Drop by teaspoonfuls onto the cookie sheets, spacing the cookies 2 inches apart. Bake, one pan at a time, on an upper shelf in the oven for 20–23 minutes, until lightly golden. Slide cookies, still on the parchment paper, onto countertop to cool.

Put the chocolate chips into a small metal bowl and place over simmering water until chocolate is melted. Dip the baked macaroons into the chocolate to cover the bottom of each macaroon. Place on waxed paper to harden.

NORWEGIAN CREAM CONES

To make these cones, you will need to use a Norwegian krumkake iron, available in most Scandinavian cookware shops or online. The cones can be made several days in advance of serving, but must be stored in an airtight container to retain their crispness.

MAKES ABOUT 36

Cones:
½ cup sugar
4 tablespoons (½ stick) butter, softened
1 large egg, at room temperature
½ cup milk
¾ cup all-purpose flour

Whipped Cream Filling (recipe follows)

In a medium-sized bowl, cream the sugar with the butter. Beat in the egg until the mixture is light. Beat in the milk and flour until blended and smooth. Let stand 30 minutes.

Preheat a Norwegian krumkake iron and coat with cooking spray. Once the cone batter has rested for 30 minutes, spoon 1 teaspoonful of the batter onto the center of the iron. Close the iron and cook for 15 seconds until the cookie is golden brown. Remove and quickly turn into a cone shape. Place upright in a stemmed wine glass or a sundae dish to retain the cone shape while the cookie cools. Repeat with the rest of the batter.

Whipped Cream Filling:
½ cup whipping cream
3 tablespoons powdered sugar

For the filling, whip the cream until stiff and add the powdered sugar. When the cones are cool, fill them with Whipped Cream Filling just before serving.

INDEX

Page numbers in italic indicate photos.

almonds
  almond paste in Mincemeat Filling, 55
  Almond Pastry, 53
  Chocolate-Dipped Almond Biscotti, 139
  Swedish Almond Tarts, 58
Angel Cakes with Lemon Sauce, 18, 19
Applesauce Crisp, 62, 63
Apricot Filling, 66
Apricot Schaum Tortelets, 64, 65–66

Baby Rum Babas, 33–34, 35
bananas in Vanilla Banana Cream Pies, 45, 47
Biscotti, Chocolate-Dipped Almond, 139
Biscuits, 68
Bittersweet Espresso Chocolate Brownie Bites, 39
blueberries
  Blueberry Cobblerettes, 67–68
  Blueberry Dollar Cakes, 72, 73
Bread Puddings, Miniature, 106–07
Butter Pastry, 129

cakes
  Angel Cakes with Lemon Sauce, 19
  Baby Rum Babas, 33–34
  Bittersweet Espresso Chocolate Brownie Bites, 39
  Cardamom-Spiced Currant Cakes, 21
  Chocolate Velvet Cakes, 12
  Coconut Rum Butter Cakes, 25
  Coffee Chocolate Rolls, 31
  Fresh Ginger Carrot Cakelets, 15
  Mini Cheesecakes with Berries and Fruit, 28
  Sponge Cake, 27
  Whoopie Pies, 37–38
Calliope Coffee, 90, 91
Caramel Drizzle, 32
caramels in Dulce de Leche Cream Puffs, 128
Cardamom-Spiced Currant Cakes, 21, 23
carrots in Fresh Ginger Carrot Cakelets, 15
Chai Panna Cotta, 86
Cheesecakes with Berries and Fruit, Mini, 29
Cherries, Chocolate-Dipped, 77
chilled desserts See also mousses; Panna Cottas
  Calliope Coffee, 91
chocolate
  Bittersweet Espresso Chocolate Brownie Bites, 39
  Chocolate Banana Cream Pies, 47
  Chocolate Drizzle, 32
  Chocolate Espresso Mousse, 88, 89
  Chocolate Filling, 32
  Chocolate Glaze, 136
  Chocolate Hazelnut Éclairs, 135–36, 137
  Chocolate Hazelnut Filling, 136
  Chocolate Soufflés, 105
  Chocolate Truffle Filling, 52
  Chocolate Truffle Tarts, 50, 51, 52
  Chocolate Velvet Cakes, 12, 13
  Chocolate-Dipped Almond Biscotti, 138, 139
  Chocolate-Dipped Cherries, 76, 77
  Coconut Ginger Macaroons, 140
  Coffee Chocolate Rolls, 31
  Crispy Cream Puffs, 127
  Espresso Chocolate Frosting, 39
  Italian Ricotta and Fruit Filled Cream Puffs, 125
  Milk Chocolate Panna Cotta, 86
  Mocha Rum Pots de Crème, 117–18
  White Chocolate Mousse, 95
  Whoopie Pies, 37–38
Choux Paste, 129–30 See also cream puffs
Classic Crème Brûlée, 108, 109
Coconut Ginger Macaroons, 140, 141
Coconut Rice Pudding, 101

Coconut Rum Butter Cakes, 24, 25
Coconut Rum Sauce, 26
coffee
  Calliope Coffee, 91
  Chocolate Espresso Mousse, 88
  Coffee Chocolate Rolls, 30, 31
  Espresso Chocolate Frosting, 39
  Mocha Rum Pots de Crème, 117–18
Cones, Norwegian Cream, 143
Cranberry Sauce, 100
cream cheese
  Cream Cheese Frosting, 15
  Cream Cheese pastry, 49
  Creamy Filling, 74
  Creamy Pumpkin Mini Mousses, 82, 83
  Mini Cheesecakes with Berries and Fruit, 28
  Ricotta Cranberry Custard, 99
Cream Filling, 130
cream puffs
  Chocolate Hazelnut Éclairs, 135
  Crispy Cream Puffs, 127
  Dulce de Leche Cream Puffs, 128
  Italian Ricotta and Fruit Filled Cream Puffs, 125
  Mini Cream Puffs, 124
  Miniature Swedish Maria Pastries, 129–30
crème brûlées
  Classic Crème Brûlée, 108
  Hazelnut Crème Brûlée, 112
  Rhubarb Crème Brûlée, 110–11
Crepes Suzette See Orange Crepes
Crisp Topping, 62
Crispy Cream Puffs, 127
Crispy Meringues, 45
Currant Cakes, Cardamom-Spiced, 21
custards and puddings
  Coconut Rice Pudding, 101
  Miniature Bread Puddings, 106–07
  Mocha Rum Pots de Crème, 117–18
  Pumpkin Cream Pots, 102
  Ricotta Cranberry Custard, 99
  Vanilla Pots de Crème, 113–14

Dobos Torte See Coffee Chocolate Rolls
Dulce de Leche Cream Puffs, 128

Éclairs, Chocolate Hazelnut, 135–36
Espresso Chocolate Frosting, 39

fillings
  Apricot Filling, 66
  Chocolate Filling, 32
  Chocolate Hazelnut Filling, 136
  Chocolate Truffle Filling, 52
  Cream Filling, 130
  Creamy Filling, 74
  Lemon Filling, 57
  Lime Filling, 44
  Maple Pecan Filling, 49
  Marshmallow Filling, 38
  Mincemeat Filling, 55
  Vanilla Cream Filling, 47
  Whipped Cream Filling, 143
Frango, Frozen Maple, 120, 121
Fresh Ginger Carrot Cakelets, 15, 17
Fresh Ginger Ice Cream, 119
Fresh Lime Pies, 42, 43
Fresh Raspberry Shooters, 78, 79
frostings See also toppings
  Cream Cheese Frosting, 15
  Decorative Icing, 55
  Espresso Chocolate Frosting, 39
  Vanilla Frosting, 14
frozen desserts See Frango, Frozen Maple; Ice Cream, Fresh Ginger
Fruit Topping, 28

gelatin, 91
  Calliope Coffee, 90
  Mango Mousse, 92
  Orange and Ginger Panna Cotta, 87
  Panna Cotta Three Ways, 85–86
ginger
  Coconut Ginger Macaroons, 140
  Fresh Ginger Carrot Cakelets, 15
  Fresh Ginger Ice Cream, 119
  Orange and Ginger Panna Cotta, 87
graham crackers in Fresh Lime Pies, 42
Greek-Style Honey-Nut Pastries, 132, 133–34

hazelnuts
  Chocolate Hazelnut Éclairs, 135–36
  Hazelnut Crème Brûlée, 112
honey
  Greek-Style Honey-Nut Pastries, 133–34
  Honey Syrup, 134

Ice Cream, Fresh Ginger, 119
icings See frostings
Italian Ricotta and Fruit Filled Cream Puffs, 125, 126

jams and jellies
  Strawberry Topping, 74
  Swedish Almond Tarts, 58

lemons
  lemon curd in Lemon Filling, 57
  Lemon Sauce, 20
Lime Pies, Fresh, 42
liqueurs
  Orange Syrup, 70
  Vanilla Pots de Crème, 113–14

Macaroons, Coconut Ginger, 140
Mango Mousse, 92, 93
maple syrup
  Frozen Maple Frango, 120
  Maple Pecan Pies, 48, 49
Marshmallow Filling, 38
mascarpone cheese in Lemon Filling, 57
Meringue, 57
Milk Chocolate Panna Cotta, 86
Mincemeat Filling, 55
Mini Cheesecakes with Berries and Fruit, 28, 29
Mini Cream Puffs, 124
Mini Mince Pies, 53, 54
Miniature Bread Puddings, 106–07
Miniature Swedish Maria Pastries, 129–30, 131
Mocha Rum Pots de Crème, 116, 117–18
mousses
  Chocolate Espresso Mousse, 88
  Creamy Pumpkin Mini Mousses, 82
  Mango Mousse, 92
  White Chocolate Mousse, 95

Norwegian Cream Cones, 142, 143
nuts See specific nuts

oranges
  Orange and Ginger Panna Cotta, 87
  Orange Crepes, 69, 71
  Orange Syrup, 70

pancakes
  Blueberry Dollar Cakes, 73
  Orange Crepes, 69–70
Panna Cottas
  Orange and Ginger Panna Cotta, 87
  Panna Cotta Three Ways, 84, 85–86
Pecan Pies, Maple, 49
Petite Lemon Meringue Pies, 56

phyllo dough in Greek-Style Honey-Nut Pastries, 133–34
Pie Crust Decorations, 104
pies and tarts
  Chocolate Truffle Tarts, 50, 52
  Fresh Lime Pies, 42
  Maple Pecan Pies, 49
  Mini Mince Pies, 53
  Petite Lemon Meringue Pies, 56
  Swedish Almond Tarts, 58
  Tart Pastry, 50, 52
  Vanilla Banana Cream Pies, 45, 47
puddings and Pots de Crème See custards and puddings
pumpkin
  Creamy Pumpkin Mini Mousses, 82
  Pumpkin Cream Pots, 102, 103, 104

Raspberry Shooters, Fresh, 78
Red Velvet Cake See Chocolate Velvet Cakes
Rhubarb Crème Brûlée, 110–11
Rice Pudding, Coconut, 101
ricotta cheese
  Italian Ricotta and Fruit Filled Cream Puffs, 125
  Ricotta Cranberry Custard, 98, 99
rum
  Baby Rum Babas, 33–34
  Coconut Rum Butter Cakes, 25
  Coconut Rum Sauce, 26
  Mocha Rum Pots de Crème, 117–18
  Rum Syrup, 34

Sandbakkelser See Swedish Almond Tarts
sauces See toppings
Soufflés, Chocolate, 105
Sponge Cake, 27
Sponge Cake rusks, 74
Strawberry Bruschetta, 74, 75
Strawberry Topping, 74
Sugar Topping, 22
Swedish Almond Tarts, 58, 59
Syrup, Honey, 134

tarts See pies and tarts
tea in Chai Panna Cotta, 86
toppings See also frostings
  Caramel Drizzle, 32
  Chocolate Drizzle, 32
  Chocolate Glaze, 136
  Coconut Rum Sauce, 26
  Cranberry Sauce, 100
  Cream Glaze, 127
  Crisp Topping, 62
  Dulce de Leche Sauce, 128
  Fruit Topping, 28
  Lemon Sauce, 20
  Orange Syrup, 70
  Rum Syrup, 34
  Strawberry Topping, 74
  Sugar Topping, 22

Vanilla Banana Cream Pies, 45, 46
Vanilla Frosting, 14
Vanilla Panna Cotta, 85
Vanilla Pots de Crème, 113–14, 115
vanilla wafers
  Mini Cheesecakes with Berries and Fruit, 28
  Vanilla Banana Cream Pies, 45, 47

walnuts in Greek-Style Honey-Nut Pastries, 133–34
Whipped Cream Filling, 143
White Chocolate Mousse, 94, 95
Whoopie Pies, 36, 37–38
wine in Fresh Raspberry Shooters, 78